IT GROWS ON YOU

A
HAIR-RAISING
SURVEY
OF
HUMAN
PLUMAGE

IT GROWS ON YOU

A HAIR-RAISING SURVEY OF HUMAN PLUMAGE

■

BY
ROY BLOUNT, JR.

■

PHOTOGRAPHS
BY
BOB ADELMAN

 A DOLPHIN BOOK, DOUBLEDAY & COMPANY, INC., GARDEN CITY, NEW YORK • 1986

A BOB ADELMAN BOOK

DESIGN: BOB CIANO
PHOTO EDITOR: HAZEL HAMMOND
PRODUCTION: DAYNA BURNETT
PHOTOGRAPHIC PRINTS: DAVID ZICKL
TYPOGRAPHY: U.S. LITHOGRAPH, TYPOGRAPHERS

The authors would like to thank all the people pictured in the book for their collaboration. We would also like to thank Brigitte Grosjean, Andrew Finkelstein, Jane Gelb, Jack Shor and Karen Fisher for their assistance.

Frontispiece. Hair design sign, Los Angeles.
Page 8. Teressa O'Neil models Schumi Schapers, which curl her hair.
Page 11. Split ends in Paris.
Pages 12-15. Author's hair over the years.
Pages 16, 17. Author hooked up to a Van Der Graf generator.
Page 50. Judge Charles L. Brieant.
Page 52. Married couple from Washington, D.C.
Page 54. Gay Pride parade, Los Angeles.
Pages 58, 74, 75. Glenda, hair stylist at Saks.
Page 62. Hair show participant at New York dance club.
Page 64. Windblown hair in Tulsa.
Pages 68, 72, 73. Bridget LeRoy.
Page 95. Instructor at Glemby's beauty school.
Pages 124, 125, 126. Hal Martin Jacobs.
Page 142. John Sex says he has the world's tallest pompadour.

Library of Congress Cataloging-in-Publication Data
Blount, Roy.
   It grows on you.
   "A Dolphin book."
   1. Hair—Anecdotes, facetiae, satire, etc.
I. Adelman, Bob. II. Title.
QP88.3.B56 1986   646.7'24'0207   86-16682
ISBN 0-385-23034-6

CONTENTS

1. Just a Little Off the Top—and in Trouble Already 9

Astor Place

2. What *Is* Hair, Why Do We *Have* It, What Is the Deal Here? 25

Hairs Blown Up Enormously
Hair in the Sixties
Hair in the Family
Believe It or Not
Just One Brush With Whiskers
Accustomed Though He May Have Been to a Bit of Mustache
Notes on Androgyny

3. Getting Folk Beliefs by the Short Hairs 59

4. Talking to Women About Their Hair 67

Romantic Hair Gestures Among the Literati
It's the Little Things

5. Cutters and Shapers 83

Kenneth
Louis Licari
Vittorio
Champion Barbershop
Industrial Hair
Mr. Kay
Hair Show
Beauty School
"Wahoo Sam" Crawford
Taking Hair into Your Own Hands

6. Shampoo and Other Gunk 101

Hair Testing
Loose Ends

7. You Know How to Avoid Falling Hair? Step Aside 121

Wigmaker, Raffaele
You Think You Have Problems?

8. Street Hair 132

New York
London

9. Pulling It All Together: The Hair Theory of Human Evolution 143

Makeover

Glossary 154
Questions for Further Study 156
Answers to Questions for Further Study 158

This one's for Esther—*not* because it's short—and for the
Alligator Point boys, because they're coarse.
—R.B.

For Samantha. And for David, whose hair is about the
same length.
—B.A.

Parmenides: Are you also puzzled, Socrates, about cases that might be thought absurd, such as hair or mud or dirt or any other trivial and undignified objects? . . . .

Socrates: Not at all. In these cases, the things are just the things we see; it would surely be too absurd to suppose that they have a form. All the same, I have sometimes been troubled by a doubt . . . . Then, when I have reached that point, I am driven to retreat, for fear of tumbling into a bottomless pit of nonsense.

Changing our hair is probably the most effective alteration that any of us can perform.

> —*Look Like a Winner; Why, When and Where to Wear What*
> by Lee Hogan Cass and Karen E. Anderson

I could a tale unfold whose lightest word
Would harrow up thy soul, freeze thy young blood,
Make thy two eyes, like stars, start from their spheres,
Thy knotted and combined locks to part
And each particular hair to stand on end.

> —*the Ghost to Hamlet*

Sometimes, you like to let the hair do the talking.

> —*James Brown*

CHAPTER ONE

JUST A LITTLE OFF THE TOP— AND IN TROUBLE ALREADY

The woman—her head studied yet slightly askew, shaggy-on-purpose yet a little *off*—becomes more and more highly aroused as the group discussion proceeds: hair problems, hair dreams, hair mysteries. Another woman is asked what she does first after her hair has been done.

"Oh," the other woman says, matter-of-factly, "I always cry."

The shaggy woman stands, flushed, tired of all this beating around the bush. "I *am* my hair," she cries.

No, that's not the way to begin.

"When I see a person," says a barber in New Haven, Connecticut, "I see his potential hairstyle. Some barbers are very formulaic about the way they cut hair. I just sort of jump on the head and start working. I'm always experimenting, though I usually pretend I know exactly what I'm doing."

No, that's not the way to begin either. I could never be a barber. I'm not enough into control. I *know* what *everyone's* potential hairstyle looks like, essentially, because I saw it in *An Illustrated Dictionary of Hairdressing and Wigmaking*, in a bookstore in Oxford, England. And my blood ran cold. And at the same time I saw the light (so to speak)....

Excuse this book, I know it's a mess. I mean verbally, structurally, deep down. Yes, I'm sure it does *look* nice; thank you. But if you only knew the thin spots, the cowlicks, the wandering parts, the *loss*, the stray leads. Things keep popping up! This morning I found a little note to myself: "Elisha/baldness/she-bears/rough and smooth." It fell out of *Bébé, The Films of Brigitte Bardot* (you talk about *hair*), and I knew it didn't belong there, but all I could do was tuck it back in. In the words of Warren Beatty, in *Shampoo*, "I'm losing all my concepts!" But I must hold on—as the prince clung to Rapunzel's hair, and climbed—to this book's one great wave or thread, which came to me, ironically enough (not that anything ever really is), when I saw that horrible illustration in Oxford:

That—though hair is not fair and we might as well face up to it....

That hair—though it's *dead*; you *can't* "nourish" or "heal" it; it is strings of deceased protein flecks, excreted by the follicles (and what a jaunty word, *follicle*: comes from the same root as *fool*)....

That human hair, ironically enough (for now), is—against its will, presumably; I mean a dead thing doesn't have any will unless it's a ghost, which may be what hair is....

That human head hair, though its natural tendency, except in moments of terror, is down, down, down....

That this run-amuck vestige of fur atop the human cranium is uplifting; that hair is what raised our prehistoric forebears into humanity (erection, manufacture, reflection, horizon-gazing, love)....

And that it's still a mess.

You can read all the books, shampoo ads and *Vogue* advisories you want, about how to make your hair work, how to succeed through your hair, how to give your hair more richness, fullness, vibrancy....

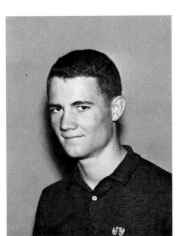

But how about all of us who look at the photographs in those books and think, But pictures of hair are not hair. And then look at our own hair and think, Why doesn't other people's hair look like this?

It does. This is the book that tells you it does, and worse. You can't imagine how bad some people's hair looks. There is no way of looking bad that hair hasn't tried.

This is a book about how crazy hair is. What a crazy material, what a crazy proposition, with what a crazy history. A crazy mess—lifeless, growing, snarling, beguiling, entwining us with seducers and hairdressers. It's all over our heads, an eighth of an inch from our minds. A mess.

And yet. . . .

You know the Southern expression, "Aren't you a *mess*"?

A mess in that sense is a flatterer, a kidder, a caution, a cutie; up to something.

"But you're a man," you say, if you're a woman. "What do *you* know?"

Ah, let me tell you.

The other day I saw a woman enter a restaurant and exclaim to a man waiting for her, "I look like the *Donna Reed Show*! I hate my hair more than I ever have in my life!" Eavesdropping, I gathered that she had just had her hair cut, by someone recommended by this guy's mother. This guy had his dinner conversation cut out for him.

But it's not only women's hair that men get caught up in. The truth is that men (even if, like an old football coach I heard about, their policy is to keep it so short "I don't have to wash or comb it, I just wipe it off with a rag") have hair on the brain, too.

Let us take a man who has been through all the hair changes of the last forty years. Call him Harry.

First Harry had to brave the barbershop when he was a little kid. Maybe his father thought it smelled good in there, but what was all that stuff? Wildroot and Lucky Tiger and bay rum and witch hazel—and they're waving straight razors around in there, and there's this terrible electric-clipper drone whose vibes are so low Harry can feel them in his molars. And old creaky guys are cracking jokes Harry doesn't understand (and they *know* he doesn't understand), and they have hair growing out of their *noses*. Out of their *ears*.

Then Harry approaches puberty and he realizes that what these old creaky barbers really want to do is not to cut his ears off (in spite of all those jokes they told about the barber who kept a dog next to the chair, waiting....) but to expose them horribly—to make him look like a dork. The one thing he does not want to happen, always happens.

Which is this: when E.B. pops his apron—if that's what you call it, the sheet he puts over you to keep the falling hair from getting on you.... When E.B. pops his apron, *pop*, Harry is always next.

E.B. is the barber who, no matter what you tell him (and whatever you tell him you sound like a sissy), gives you a white wall.

Troglodyte son of a bitch.

Against all the odds, Harry tries to be stylish. He gets a flattop, but his hair is too fine to stay erect so he strokes stiffener into it and that doesn't work either, and the other guys are peroxiding their hair in front, so he does too, and it comes out green and his mother never gets over it. (She already will never get over his first haircut. She keeps bringing up the golden curls God gave Harry when he was little and sweet.) He tries ducktails, but he is not a hood at heart (he realizes with shame) and anyway his hair is too curly (in this strange way that nobody else's is) to stay greased in place.

Then when Harry is in college he goes into a bit of a hippie stage, lets his hair keep growing—as they sang in *Hair*—"till it stops by itself." It may stop growing by itself, but it never stops getting messy by itself or even with help, and now instead of a sketchy mess it's a huge mess. It looks like this enormous, dirty, asymmetrical *mushroom*. He finds himself tossing his head and brushing hair out of his eyes the way women do. His hair is just as natural as Adam's, and yet it's this big production all the time. And gas station guys call him "Ma'am" and proletarians want to beat him up because he looks like a Communist.

And he gets drafted and they make him look like a dork again.

And he gets out and goes to work and there are certain ways a young man who works where he works really ought to keep his hair trim if the old guys there are going to like the cut of his jib, and certain other ways he has to let it loosen up if he is ever going to get anywhere with women. And then there are all these new mousses and gels for men that some guys seem to know how to use so that their hair looks like it just naturally grows orderly yet bouncy—but these mousses and gels do not work for Harry. These mousses and gels make Harry look like someone with mousse and gel on his head. And can he ask other guys how they use mousse and gel? No. He is a man.

And Harry's hair starts coming out.

And now that he is trying to get enough body into his hair to balance incipient jowls, and is trying to train some of that body over to cover the thin spots—do you know what the hot hair look for men is now, now that Harry is too old to carry it off?

Dorky.

I am not, in every respect, Harry. I am not balding, and therefore have little sympathy for men who are obsessed with that problem. (Which we will, however, take up in these pages.) I don't work in an office, and therefore am content to be scruffy —except sometimes when I see myself on television and say, "Good Lord." I am no more upset about my inability to look New Wave than I am about my almost total ignorance of ice hockey.

And yet I begin every day of my life shaken by the sight of my hair.

I don't care what length it is, or how good or recent a haircut I have, I always sleep on my hair wrong. Very wrong. I look at myself in the mirror and there is my hair, looking as if it has been pasted on, hurriedly, crankily, by a nursery-school class.

Tousled? Hey, tousled I could live with. Tousled is about the best I achieve. But my hair in the morning is not just disorderly. It is unpleasant. It suggests pond trash, old road-kills, half-masticated straw, here and there an outcropping of failed— no, twisted—soufflé.

I don't mousse. I don't even blow-dry. But I do, every morning of my life, have to shampoo, condition and comb, and wait until the right time to put my cap on, and think about getting another damn haircut pretty soon in order not to look like scum.

Do you know why I am unsympathetic to men who complain about baldness? Because I think I could get into it.

"But wait a minute," you say. "Aren't you ignoring a whole class of people? All those people who don't think hair is a mess? How about all those people with naturally good hair?"

People with good hair don't read.

ASTOR PLACE

The young assemble in great clumps on the sidewalk outside New York's Astor Place Hair Designers, because you can get any cut you want in there, for $8 and up. If you want to dance, you go to a dance club. If you want a cut, you go to the Astor Place. If you've decided you want your head to look sort of like a pineapple, you appreciate a supportive atmosphere. The Astor Place barbers work very fast, and may leave a hair hanging here and there, but what do you want, a *leisurely* punk cut? Your friends can pull out the odd long hair, after you've looked at each other and gasped, in a cool way, and laughed out loud.

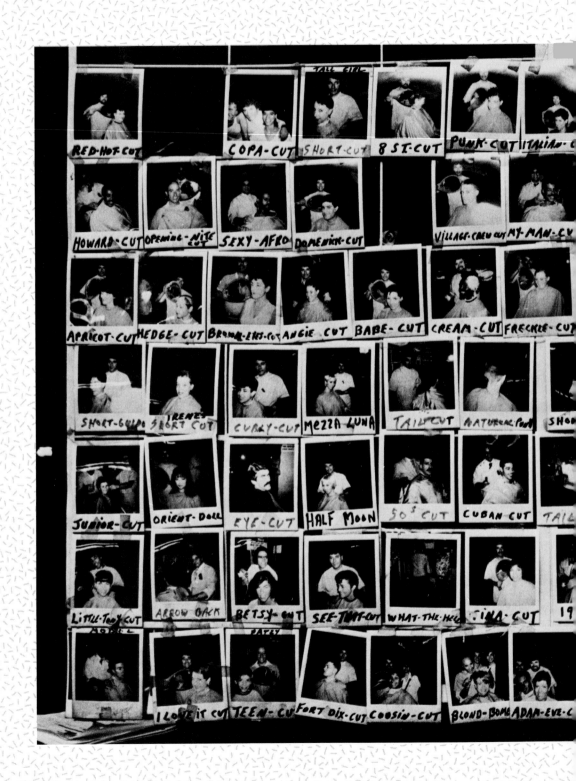

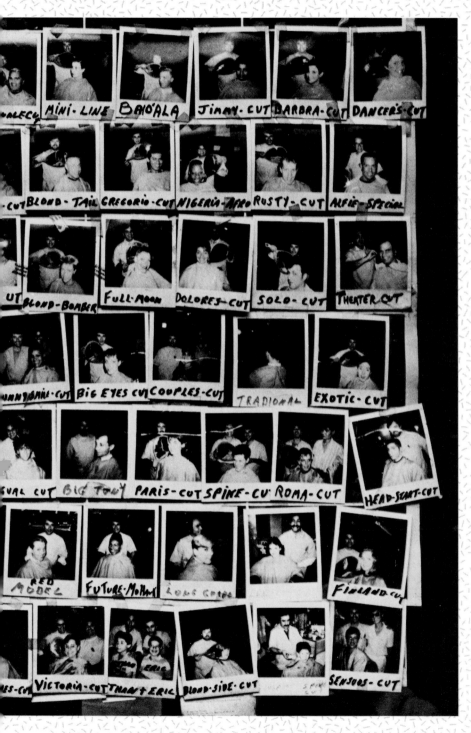

You can also get an LA-Cut, a TV-Cut, a Cute-Cut, a Monk-Cut, a Detroit-Cut, a Photo-Cut, a Feather-Cut, a Beauty-Cut, a Long Crew, an Aunt-Cut, an Apollo-Cut, a Lamp-Cut, a Special-Cut, an Oh-Shit-Cut, a Khan-Cut, a Wild-Ones-Cut, a Hazel-Eyes-Cut, a Pretty-Cut, a Fort-Dix-Cut, a Long Guido, a See-That-Cut, an Opening-Nite-Cut, a Red-Hot-Cut, an Apricot-Cut, a Sparkle-Cut, a Hedge-Cut, a Spina di Pesce. And many others.

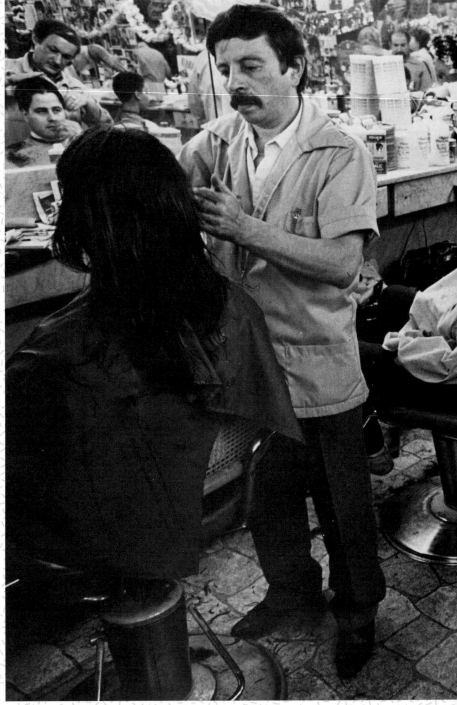

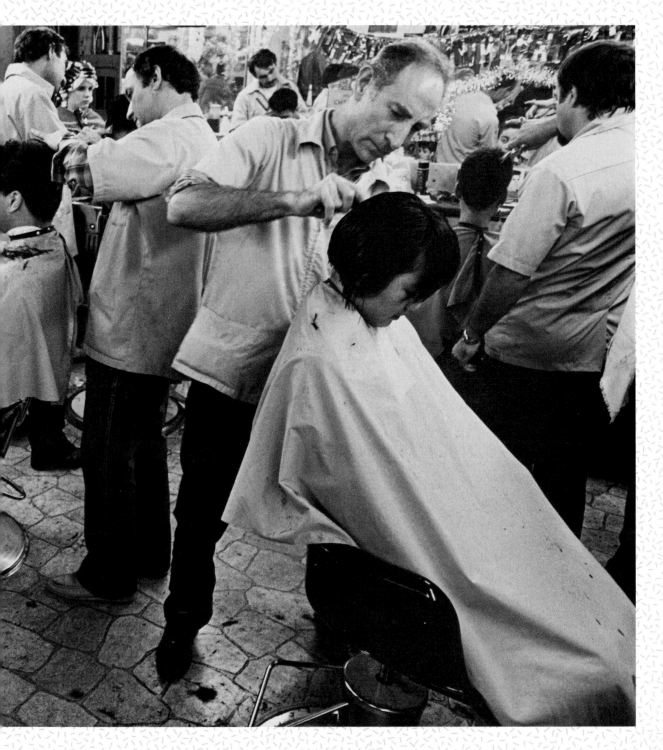

CHAPTER TWO
WHAT *IS* HAIR, WHY DO WE *HAVE* IT, WHAT IS THE DEAL HERE?

One hair is a prickle, an abomination in the butter. A lock of it is a totem, a charm, a memento mori. A shock of it can be so soft. A full, developed, tended flow of it is a crown of glory. And a pain in the ass to maintain.

This is from the *American Heritage Dictionary*:

1a. One of the cylindrical often pigmented filaments characteristically growing from the epidermis of a mammal. *b.* A growth of such filaments, as that forming the coat of an animal or covering the scalp of a human being.

The movement there is nice, from cylindrical filament to coat. Words can move more mysteriously than film. So can hair.

The wind messes it up, and so do the atmosphere and our glands. It acts like it wants to be a hank, or a rat's nest, or to drop out. But we can do something with it. There is only so much, short of drastic measures, that we can change about our mouths or hands, but our hair we instinctively feel we ought to be able to handle. We can use it to express ourselves, not in the sense that we use our eyes to express ourselves but in the sense that we use clothes or watercolors. And we can use it to hide ourselves around the edges.

SOME NICE HAIR LINES—1

"David [played by Albert Brooks in the movie *Lost in America*] has a bland moonface surrounded by an aureole of tight dark curls; it's as if he wore his brains on the outside."

—Pauline Kael, *The New Yorker*

And it will grow out. Our faces or our minds won't. Maybe they will grow into something, but they won't keep returning as raw material. And we can't change them readily. We can do something to our hair right now, something drastic. We are always fooling with it.

And making a big deal of it. Where would art, myth and history be without hair? Without the nose we wouldn't have what? Cyrano, Pinocchio, Gogol and Jimmy Durante. Without hair we'd lose Lady Godiva, Samson and Delilah, *The Barber of Seville*, "The Rape of the Lock," "Bernice Bobs Her Hair," Rapunzel, *Sweeney Todd*, Jacob and Esau, Absalom, *Gentlemen Prefer Blondes*, Goldilocks, Rhonda Fleming, Kojack, Medusa, the sixties, Santa Claus, Little Richard, Veronica Lake, Madame Pompadour, Professor Longhair, *Struwwelpeter*, California girls, "Haircut" and angel hair pasta.

The musical about the fifties was *Grease*, the musical about the sixties was *Hair* and the movie about the seventies was *Shampoo*. (I was going to write the musical of the eighties for this book, but I guess I don't have room. The title was going to be *Mousse*.)

The sexiest Christian scene is Mary Magdalene drying Jesus' feet with her hair. And show me a nose myth that can come up to this: when Osiris died without issue, Isis warmed his body with her hair until his heart turned over and his penis moved "and she drew essence from him, she made flesh and blood," and then she warmed the child by "shaking out her hair over him."

Another way in which the nose differs from hair is that we know what the nose is for. Scientists can't account for human hair. They speculate that we have so little fur, not because the wearing of animal skins wore it off or made it unnecessary, but because humanity began in tropical Africa and early man, being carnivorous but no tiger, had to stalk his prey for hours in the hot sun and therefore had to doff fur to avoid sunstroke. That's what they speculate. At any rate, all those illustrations of cavemen getting less hairy by stages as they get less apelike are pure speculation; since hair does not survive in the fossil record, we have no way of knowing whether Neanderthal was more hirsute than Cro-Magnon.

But why is what fur we do have concentrated in our most out-of-the-way (well, that's not quite the word) places and our most public? Crotch and armpit hair may have some cushioning function. Nose hair keeps dirt out and nose-run in. Eyebrows keep sweat out of the eyes and cut down on glare. Eyelashes keep grit out of the eyes. (Camels have a double set of eyelashes, for sand. You may not be surprised to learn that camels also have a lot of hair in their noses.)

And head hair presumably protected early man's brain from the sun. But it has been millennia since we've had to depend on head hair to provide much in the way of protection, and it doesn't provide much anyway, and it certainly doesn't have to grow so long for reasons of protection. And yet it thrives, keeps pouring out. Why does the body keep requiring the follicles to send up these troublesome, scaly tubes of protein? Why doesn't the body just buy itself a hat?

One theory is that hair's sole evolutionary purpose is adornment. People with full heads of hair call attention to it (it's ideally suited to attention-calling), attract mates and perpetuate hirsuteness. And myths and musicals.

And some of the craziest, trashiest carrying-on you can imagine. I mean people have kept marble statues of themselves in their homes, with interchangeable marble wigs. People have held their hair in place with rotten oak paste. People have regarded other people as infidels because they were hairy and then again because they weren't. Entire male populations of defeated countries have had to cut their hair off.

Emperors whose hair fell out have passed laws requiring everyone to have short hair. People have left their wigs to people in their wills. In the eighteenth century, the British rich used up so much flour powdering their wigs that the British poor had a bread shortage.

We remember Madame Pompadour for her high, combed-back front, but her hairdo also involved wire frames, bushels of cotton wool, shreds of rope, horsehair and bran. The whole thing was cemented with a paste that hardened into an outer shell, which was greased, floured and decorated with gauze, tulle and pearls. And left that way for two to nine weeks. An anti-wig poet of the day wrote:

> When he scents the mingled steam
> Which your plaster'd heads are rich in,
> Lard and meal, and clouted cream,
> Can he love a walking kitchen?

Colley Cibber, the eighteenth-century English writer and actor, had a wig so big that men had to carry it onstage in a sedan chair.

On the other hand, Samuel Sewall of Massachusetts, who was virtuous enough in his own right that he felt it behooved him to sentence women to death as witches, fought against wigs as "godless emblems of iniquity." When a Boston wig-maker died, Sewall wrote in his diary with relish: "This day Wm. Clendon the . . . Perriwig-maker, dies miserably, being almost eat up with lice and stupified with Drink and cold."

One day Marie Antoinette hummed a tune from an opera, and within days ladies of the court were wearing scenes from that opera in their hair.

At the turn of the twentieth century, seven farm girls from upstate New York, the seven Sutherland sisters, gave it to be known that they had the longest hair in the world—a total of thirty-six feet, ten inches among them—and that they owed it

In their glory, the seven Sutherland sisters. And one of them close up.

all to the Seven Sutherland Sisters' Hair Grower and Scalp Cleaner, which their father, Fletcher Sutherland, mixed up and which some people said was rainwater and alcohol. The sisters became circus stars, whose act was to stand in a spotlight and let their hair fall down their backs. They built a mansion with marble bathrooms.

What *is* this stuff?

It's stuff that mothers and daughters share the way fathers and sons share baseball. It's stuff that girls braid for each other, that Indian widows and retiring Sumo wrestlers hack off, and that families of people in comas brush and keep on brushing, hoping the comatose can tell.

Why not feathers? Feathers develop pretty much the same way hair does; they're dead skin cells that specialize, sort of like elaborate scabs. Feathers would be neater, less trouble, less conducive to bigotry and excess, just as pretty, far more egalitarian; they hold their shape; they're useful. With feathers on our heads we'd never have to wear hats, and we might be able to lift ourselves slightly from the scalp, pick up a little hover; and basketball would be something else.

Or we could have a little cap of scales, and shed it every so often the way snakes slough off their skins: organized dandruff.

But no, our heads have to yield this preposterous crop. Some lizards and insects have hairline projections, but only mammals have true hair. And only human beings have cranial growth that goes on and on and on. A human scalp hair may grow from half an inch to an inch every month for up to six years. That adds up to seventy-two inches.

Trees don't grow leaves that get out of hand like that. Rhinoceroses don't grow horns so headstrong. A lion's mane is content. Human head hair is by far the most runaway appendage in nature. It just keeps on coming. Why? Why? Why?

I'm going to tell you. All in good time.

WHY YOU SHOULD LISTEN TO YOUR MOTHER WHEN SHE TELLS YOU NOT TO GO TO BED WITH YOUR HAIR WET

And my introduction to opium arose in the following way: From an early age I had been accustomed to wash my head in cold water at least once a day; being suddenly seized with tooth ache, I attributed it to some relaxation caused by an accidental intermission of that practice, jumped out of bed, plunged my head into a basin of cold water, and with hair thus wetted, went to sleep. The next morning, as I need hardly say, I awoke with excruciating rheumatic pains of the head and face, from which I had hardly any respite for about twenty days. On the twenty-first day I think it was, and on a Sunday, that I went out into the streets, rather to run away if possible from my torments than with any distinct purpose. By accident I met a college acquaintance who recommended opium. Opium!"

—from *Confessions of an English Opium-Eater*,
by Thomas De Quincey,
who became a lifelong addict and had
to earn a living from journalism

HAIRS BLOWN UP ENORMOUSLY

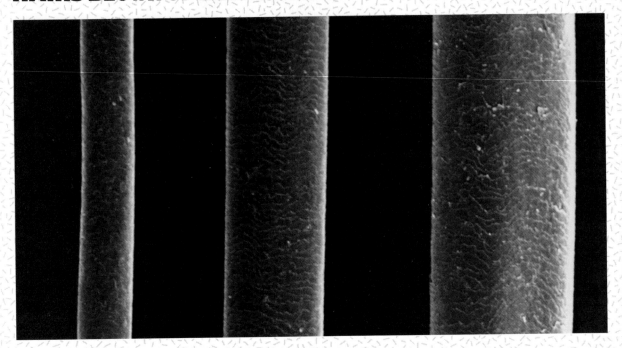

Above, the three types of hair widthwise: fine, medium and coarse. Quite a bit of difference! No wonder there's such a wide range of human personality and shampoos. Adult human nose widths don't vary that much do they? I'd be very much surprised.

Right, a hair that has been pulled out by its root. Or more precisely, by its follicle. The follicle has dried out after removal from the scalp and doesn't look the way it looked while embedded in the moist environment of the dermis. But you couldn't see it down in there.

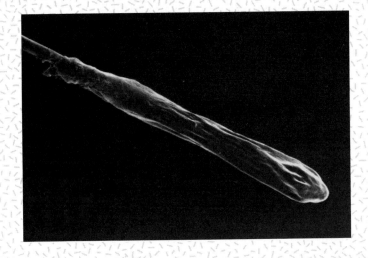

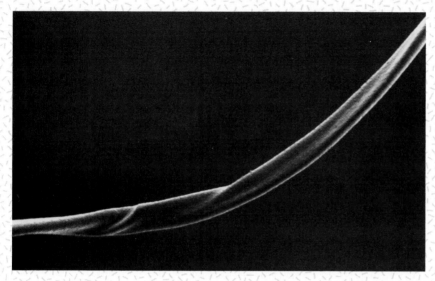

A curly hair with a twist. If you find a curly hair in your soup that doesn't have a twist, don't complain. The twist is an extra feature that the folks at the Clairol labs thought you might like to see. But all naturally curly hairs are relatively flat, like this. In case you want to check somebody out.

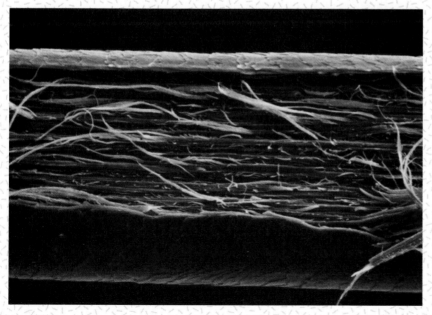

Scientists split this hair. On purpose. That's what scientists do. You can see the micro- and macrofibrils that make up the hair cortex. Yes, it does look something like an asparagus. That's what everyone says except scientists.

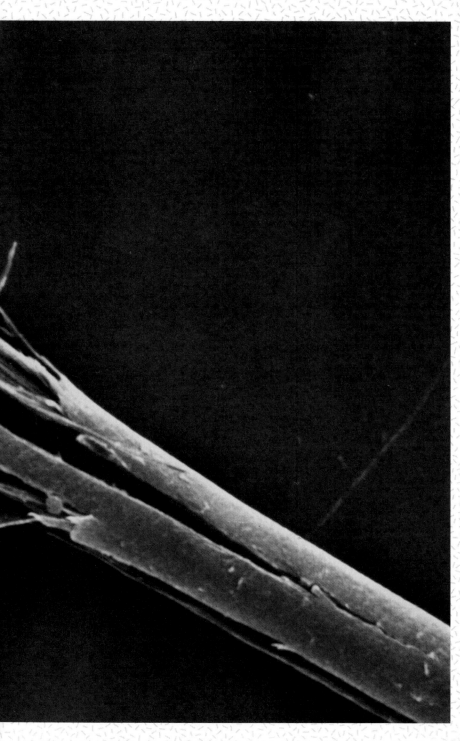

You may not want to look at this. A split end. And don't blame this one on the scientists. The average American inflicts just such damage on his or her hair every day, by means of what is known as "hair care": shampooing, setting, spraying, combing, brushing, getting burrs and chewing gum out. Just be glad the average American's hair is not magnified hundreds of times.

HAIR IN THE SIXTIES

According to Boston barber John Dellaria, the 1960s produced "a whole generation of men who said, 'I don't want to look like my dad anymore.' "

There was a caustic TV host, Joe Pine, whose practice was to have guests on his show and berate them. He had Frank Zappa on, and said, "I guess your long hair makes you a girl."

Zappa replied, "I guess your wooden leg makes you a table."

"It was hair, not only the musical announcing the Age of Aquarius, but wreathing the face and flowing down the back or, if you were black, crowning the head like an inverted bowl shaped from the strands of dreams."

—Julius Lester

If your hair was beyond a certain length, you couldn't get into Disneyland.

The Beatles

Who was the crucial figure in sixties hair history? (Which is to say, in sixties history.)

Astrid Kirchner.

Who was she?

A German art student. And Stu Sutcliffe's girl friend.

Who was *he*?

An English art student. And a Beatle. Friend of John's who was persuaded to play bass with the group while they were getting their act together in Hamburg. Not caring much for the musical life, he soon quit. (And shortly died of a brain tumor.) But not before he met Astrid Kirchner and she talked

him into combing his hair *forward and down* and cutting it in bangs. The other lads followed suit and the Beatle cut was born.

Thus began a seismic shift. Early rock 'n roll hair—except for the forehead curl that Bill Haley and then Elvis sported —had been *up and back*. Little Richard's pompadour spurred James Brown to take his hair even higher. "And people would ask," Brown later recalled, "'Why you wear your hair so high?' And I'd tell 'em, 'So people don't say *where* he is?' but '*There* he is.'" Jerry Lee Lewis roached his waves back and up, and when he played they bounced in those directions. Chuck Berry sure didn't have *bangs*.

But the Beatles did. And when Beatlemania arose, the main thing the straight media focused on was the hair. Those early Beatle cuts look prim today (when asked what he called his hairdo, Ringo said "Arthur"), but they unleashed pent-up shagginess among the crewcut and flattopped and Ivy-trim young, and outrage among the unyoung, all over Europe and the United States. Long hair, as a cultural phenomenon, began with the Beatles.

And which *way* did hair go in the sixties? Except among the tightly curly, it went down. Further and further. To the shoulders and beyond. When hair extends upward, there are limits. (Which were reached by sixties-era black athletes. An exuberant Afro just didn't fit under a helmet—football or batting —and in basketball Dr. J. at his most glorious looked, literally, like someone playing under a cloud.) But downflowing hair goes on and on: untrammeled, drifty, musky, anything-but-uptight, unstudied, androgynous, leveling, guruish-cum-animalistic, the opposite of military.

The opposite of German, too, one would have thought. Maybe that's what Astrid had in mind.

HAIR DREAMS UNMASKED

According to *Zolar's Encyclopedia and Dictionary of Dreams*:

If you dream of being bald in the front of the head, you will be in big trouble.

If you dream of being bald in the back of the head, you will live in poverty.

If you dream of a woman going bald, you will have difficulties in love affairs.

If you dream of a baby being bald, you will enjoy love.

If you dream of having brown hair, you will be a voluptuous person.

If you dream of having a ponytail, you will have many vain desires.

If you dream of having a crewcut, you are being cheated.

If you dream of your own hair (just as a general proposition, I guess), you will have continued prosperity.

If you dream of other people's hair, your own affairs will need careful attention.

If you dream of the short hair of prisoners, you will be victorious.

If you dream of having trouble taking your hair down, you will work hard a long time.

If you dream of putting up your own hair, you will have many things on your mind.

If you dream of allowing your hair to be cut up to your ears, unhappiness is in store.

If you dream of eating hair: joy.

If you dream of hair growing from the edge of your mouth: sudden death.

If you dream of having hair as long as your body, you are being deceived by your mate.

If you dream of having a wig made by a hairdresser, danger is imminent.

If you dream of enemies being at a hairdresser, you are doomed to disappointment.

If you dream of finding hairpins of a rival woman, you will be guilty of foolish actions.

If you dream of cooking halibut, expect pregnancy in the near future.

According to *What's in a Dream*:

If you dream of being covered with hair, you are likely to indulge in vices to such an extent as will debar you from the society of refined people.

According to *The Complete Dream Book*:

If you dream of finding a hair when cutting a piece of butter and it does not disgust you, it is a fortunate omen.

THE MOST MEMORABLE HAIR SCENE IN THE HISTORY OF GREAT BRITAIN

When—after three applications of the ax—Mary, Queen of Scots' head was fully severed, the executioner held it aloft and cried, "God Save the Queen." With that the head—whose lips were said to be moving still—slipped from the auburn locks in the headsman's hands and fell to the floor of the great hall of Fotheringay. It was now evident that Mary's thick, glistening, red-golden hair had become prematurely thin and gray, and she had died in a wig. Next it was revealed that her little Skye terrier, alone of all her attendants, had managed to steal into the hall with her: the dog crept out from under skirts, ran around to the block and huddled where her head had been. The deposed lapdog would not be coaxed away, but at length was taken and washed twice, to make sure no trace of Mary's blood remained on its bushy coat, lest others of her loyalists make it a relic to rally around. The dog would not eat, and died.

HAIR IN THE FAMILY

She looked on the tress! and her heart went back
O'er the vanished scenes in life's 'wildering track. . . .
It was a tress of her mother's hair!
And she saw once more the old arm-chair,
Which had sat in the corner from day to day,
'Til the locks once raven were turning grey:
Still there in summer and wintry weather,
While the mother and chair grow old together—
And the daughter wept o'er the lock of hair,
For the mother who died in the old arm-chair.

'Twas a silken tress, half brown, half grey—
And her heart went back to that weary day,
When she clipped the lock from that forehead fair—
Now in the grave 'twas mouldering there. . . .
　　　　　　—Annie R. Blount, *Poems by Miss Blount*, 1860

Sentimental? Perhaps. But King Tut's grandmother, out of pocket for three thousand years, is now known to be who she was—because her grandson saved a lock of her hair.

Early in this century, a mummified woman was found in the tomb of Amenhotep II. It was safe to assume she had been put there around 1000 B.C., when Egyptian priests tucked a number of royal mummies away in other people's tombs after they'd been displaced from their own by grave robbers. But who was she? For many years she was known to archaeologists only as the Elder Lady.

Then scientists from the University of Michigan carefully X-rayed her. The X-ray pictures greatly resembled those taken of another mummy: King Tut's great-grandmother. The scientists also clipped a sample of the Elder Lady's hair. Among the treasures of King Tut's tomb—missed, for some reason, by grave robbers—was a locket bearing the name of Tut's great-grandmother's daughter, Queen Tiye, and containing a lock of hair. When that lock and the cutting from the Elder Lady were subjected to sophisticated testing procedures, they proved almost identical. The Elder Lady was, evidently, Tut's great-grandmother's daughter: his grandmother, whose hair he took with him to another world.

A strange story?

I found Annie R. Blount's poems in the Charleston, South

Carolina, library, quite by chance. Just happened to be looking in the card catalog under Blount. It turned out she was
from Georgia, as am I.

Until then I had never known there was an Annie R. Blount
who wrote poetry. Granted, her "Hymn to Old Age" has an
ending that might gall nonagenarians:

> Not much of grief and care, I own,
> My short young life has seen;
> And yet, I'd rather far to-night
> Be ninety than nineteen.

But I found her very readable. In "A Dream," she dreams
that her lover (whose name, I was interested to learn, was
Percy) has died, and then she wakes to learn that it is true.
And then she wakes again to learn that it isn't true; Percy's
fine; she was still dreaming when she awoke the first time.
Name me another poet who ever tried anything like that.

She often writes of death and hair:

> Clip one soft and silken ringlet
> From the forehead cold;
> For the graveyard now is claiming
> All those threads of gold.

And if I were to tell you that Annie R. Blount was my great-
grandmother's name?

It still wouldn't be as good a story as O. Henry's "The Gift
of the Magi," where the struggling young couple have such a
wonderful Christmas because they discover that he has loved
her enough to sell his watch to buy her some beautiful combs
and she has loved him enough to sell her hair to buy him a
watch chain.

Do you realize how tough it is to play in this league? Even if
I could lie right.

It's a good thing I have science—my Hair Theory of Human
Evolution—to fall back on (in due time).

BELIEVE IT OR NOT

A biochemist at the University of British Columbia has proposed that werewolves and vampires may have been nothing more than people suffering from a rare group of genetic diseases called porphyria, which cause the skin to be extremely sensitive to sunlight. Porphyria victims may become very hairy —conceivably the body's effort to protect against the sun. They are well advised not to venture outside until dark, because exposure to daylight can cause their noses to fall off and can make their lips and gums so taut that the teeth look like they are jutting out wolfishly.

These symptoms can now be prevented by injections of heme, a blood product. This biochemist has suggested that in bygone days porphyriacs may have instinctively sought heme by biting people and drinking their blood. When two siblings shared the genetic defect but only one manifested symptoms, the symptomatic one may have bitten the other, who was then shocked into developing the symptoms. "If someone drank a lot of your blood," this biochemist has said, "that would certainly be stressful."

The name of this biochemist?

David Dolphin.

Dolphins are among the tiny handful of mammals (whales, elephants, Mexican hairlesses) that are less hairy than man.

(Dolphins are also perhaps the mammal least likely to bite you. But it is the hair connection that concerns us here.)

David Dolphin.

Have you noticed that the names of people in news stories have an eerie relevance? (I once read an item about a man named Harold Virgin who had gotten into legal trouble for killing an eagle, hand to talon, that attacked him.) Or something eerily *like* relevance, if you could quite figure it out?

For instance, the executive vice-president of the National Wildlife Federation, described in a news story as one of the Reagan administration's few remaining adherents among preservation-of-nature activists, is named Jay Hair.

HAIR WILL GET YOU INTO COLLEGE

On her successful application for admission to Stanford University, Robyn Weisman (who went on to write a column in the *Stanford Daily*) answered the question "What event in your life has been most memorable to you?" as follows:

> At this moment (Oct. 30, 1982), the most memorable event of my life happened last Tuesday. A senior on the third floor of my dorm came downstairs to my room to talk with me. This girl is the type of person who can't bear to touch a dog, and if you tell her you've worn your jeans for two days without washing them, she has a near heart attack and says, "Oh, yuck!" Anyway, she was telling me about her first year at Phillips (Academy, Andover), when I noticed a top retainer entangled in her long black hair. So I said, "You know, you have a retainer caught in your hair. Is it yours?"
>
> She reacted as if she [had] seen someone's limb hacked off in some cheap horror movie. She made a gagging noise, screamed and flicked the retainer out of her hair as quickly as she could. She then said, "That was so gross. I mean my hair is a mess, but that is disgusting!"
>
> I asked her if she'd pick it up with a Kleenex. I didn't want it on my floor that much. She did this reluctantly, and then she threw it in my hallway.

HAIR IN THE MOVIES

"I don't read no papers, and don't listen to no radios either. I know the world's been shaved by a drunken barber and I don't have to read it."
—Walter Brennan in *Meet John Doe*

Jimmy Cagney and a hairdresser in *Something to Sing About*:
HD: The hair—do you always comb it that way?
JC: Why yes, yes. But I can always change it if it's important.
HD: Important! Important! The hairline. Gracious! It belongs to an entirely different face!
JC: Well fix it!
HD: Hm! So easily said! When I look at that hairline I almost cry!
JC: This pan of mine may not be anything to boast about, but I will not wear a widow's peak!

Manservant to Charles Laughton as Captain Kidd:
"Pity about the hair. Dare say you've tried everything. Bear's grease.... Prenatal influence, perhaps."

At one Academy Awards show in the sixties, Elke Sommer wore her hair in the shape of a reel of film. At another, on camera, Tuesday Weld's bouffant collapsed and fell in her face.

Jack Nicholson has said that screenwriter Carole Eastman, with whom he was romantically linked at the time, was inspired to write *Five Easy Pieces* by "seeing the wind blow through my hair."

Robert Wagner complained that the bangs he had to wear in *Prince Valiant* made him look like Jane Wyman.

Larry Fine of the Three Stooges is the one Jack Kerouac described (inadequately, in *Visions of Cody*) as "meaningless goof (though somewhat mysterious as though he was a saint in disguise, a masquerading superduper witch doctor with good intentions actually)...the bushy feathery haired one." One of the things Larry doesn't look in black-and-white is strawberry blond, but that's what his brother, Morris "Moe" Steinberg, author of *Larry: The Stooge in the Middle*, says he was.

According to Steinberg, Larry's hairstyle was created when he showed up late to rehearse a show called *A Night in Venice*. Having overslept, taken a quick shower and dashed to the theater, Larry was on his way to the dressing room to comb his hair when one of the producers, Jack Shubert, grabbed him and said, "Get on that stage, *right now*, or I make you *eat* your hair." Then Shubert went further: he seized Larry's head and rubbed it violently. "There," he said. "Now you look like a stooge. I don't want to see your hair combed again—ever."

Before, the feeling had been that Larry looked too clean-cut.

When handfuls of his thinning hair were pulled out in the movies, it was artificial hair and the sound was of sailcloth being ripped next to a microphone.

━━━━━

Colette, on a given movie queen:
"This veteran young beauty defies the crushing light. She has trained herself —with what pain!—to have eyelids that don't blink, a motionless forehead; my eyes tear on seeing her lift her statuelike gaze toward the midday sun....She sweats only slightly at the roots of her carefully waved hair...."

━━━━━

When Eddie Murphy was a boy, the kids called him "Peas." "Because I wouldn't comb my hair. It rolled up in these little balls.... They'd tease girls about me, too. 'Peas is your boyfriend, Peas is your boyfriend.' When they'd start on me with 'Peas, why is your hair...,' I'd go 'Why is your mother's hair...' Like that. You had to be quick."

━━━━━

"You wear a lot of gray," Diane K. Shah said to Cary Grant in an interview.

"I'll tell you a little secret," Cary Grant said. "If your hair falls out a bit, nobody will notice."

JUST ONE BRUSH WITH WHISKERS

With head hair alone, I have bitten off more than I can chew. But here are a few facts on whiskers:

• Jim Kern, the baseball pitcher, once said of the baseball pitcher Sparky Lyle's luxuriant handlebar mustache, "It would make a great propeller."

• A single whisker grows an average of one-fifteenth of a thousandth of an inch every day.

• The beard covers a third of a square foot and contains about 15,500 hairs—each of which, when dry, is about as strong as thin copper wire.

• There are 53.7 million American men who are wet shavers (blades and shaving cream) and 19.3 million who are dry shavers (electric razor). There are 68 million American women who are wet shavers.

• If a man collected all his whiskers from regular shaving for sixteen years, he would have enough to make a one-pound ball.

• Once the baseball pitcher Ron Reed sneaked up behind the aforementioned Sparky Lyle with a pair of scissors (while Lyle was standing next to the dugout talking to someone he hadn't seen in eighteen years) and cut off half of Lyle's mustache. "What could I do?" said Lyle. "I just went on with the conversation."

• An old Spanish expression: to proceed "with the beard on the shoulder." That is, circumspectly; looking around for ambushes.

ACCUSTOMED THOUGH HE MAY HAVE BEEN TO A BIT OF MUSTACHE

How can anyone fail to be taken, at least from a distance, by St. Wilgefortis (also known as St. Liberata and St. Uncumber), the princess of Portugal? Her father, the king, betrothed her to the king of Sicily, but she had made a vow of virginity. She prayed to be delivered, whereupon a full beard grew on her face. When the king of Sicily arrived, he backed out, and Wilgefortis's dad had her crucified. I was going to drop my daughter a little note about all this, just to let her know how some fathers are, when I read to my dismay in the *Penguin Dictionary of Saints*:

"She was accordingly represented as a bearded woman hanging on a cross. This preposterous tale...started from a misunderstanding of one of those crucifixes showing Christ wearing a long tunic."

You can believe that St. Wilgefortis was only Jesus in a dress if you want to. I say she was a girl with standards.

NOTES ON ANDROGYNY

You knew something had shifted when, in the early seventies, Ed's Barbershop changed to Ed's Unisex. When you first saw Elvis on television, did you imagine *that* happening? I know Ed didn't.

Says a friend in the South who has worked in both, "The only difference I can see now between working in a barbershop and working in a beauty parlor is a barbershop has *Playboy* and a beauty parlor has *Redbook*."

On the "Joe Franklin Show," I saw a female barbershop quartette.

On MTV I saw a singer who looked and sounded exactly like a woman, except that he had a heavy black mustache and chest hair and was singing "I want my girl."

Art Cooper, the managing editor of GQ, tells me that surveys have been taken among young men in business. Why do they spend so enormously much more than their fathers ever did on products that promise them smooth skin, all-day freshness and manageable hair?

So as to catch the eye of today's young woman?

No, most of them say.

So as to compete with today's young woman in the office.

Women on the job today, say the men, are as smart and as determined as men, and on top of all that they know how to fix themselves up, how to make themselves attractive to . . . well, I guess to older men.

So women get promoted.

So I guess there is no getting around it: aspiring male execs must learn to primp. There's a trap there, of course: what if men start polishing their nails (inefficiently, at first) at their

desks? They'll look up and women will have gotten a jump on them in the apple-polishing department.

The junior vice-president as sex object? I don't know. I don't know. It may be enough to drive the old farts out of the office, and then at last women will take over the boardrooms. And men will be spending their lunch hours picking out birthday presents for their bosses' husbands.

And you know what those presents will be.

Fragrances. Compacts. Tortoise-shell combs.

And the husbands will say, "How sweet. Did you pick this out yourself, dear?"

And the bosses will say, "Er, well . . .," and lie unconvincingly.

In other words the sexes will at last experience thoughtlessness from each other's traditional end.

And we'll all have a good cry together, and fall into each other's arms as equals. And begin to kiss and roll around.

And then we will all pull back and exclaim in unison:

"You're messing up my hair!"

TV NEWSWOMEN AND THEIR HAIR

"I am probably the least glamorous person I know. I was the person who never combed her hair in high school. It was a hallmark, a badge of honor for me not have my hair combed.... I was born with blond hair. That covers a multitude of gross grooming sins."

—Diane Sawyer

"I'm fascinated with the attention my hair gets. Too long. Too much. Cut it. Leave it alone. Don't let them touch it. Don't let them do anything to it. But the only other person whose hair gets this much attention is Ted Koppel, so I'm in good company."

—Maria Shriver

"I'm a nice person. I still go to church. Also I've grown and grown and grown. I didn't stay that little girl. I grew. I learned how to do my hair and put a little highlight in it. And I learned how to do makeup. You know, I learned that."

—Phyllis George

"On-air hair" is what TV regulars call the hairstyles they wear on camera. Ironically, such hair is the opposite of on-air as in borne like a zephyr. Since TV lights create a strange halo effect if stray hairs stand out, on-air hair is like a mold.

"It's a terrible thing," says one performer, "to feel part of your hair moving while you're on the air."

THE ROLE OF HAIR IN THE HISTORY OF XEROXING

The father of Chester Carlson, inventor of xerography, was an itinerant barber crippled by arthritis. The first really successful copier required a rotating fur brush which had to be made, by a furrier, from the belly fur of Australian rabbits. The father of Robert Grundlach, who holds 131 patents mostly involving xerography, was also an inventor but with only one patent: for Wildroot Cream Oil. Robert Grundlach spent one summer in his teens "standing over a large vat in Buffalo," as David Owen put it in the *Atlantic*, "mixing all the Wildroot Cream Oil in the world."

YOUR HAIR CAN LOOK
LIKE THIS WITH NEW

WILDROOT
CREAM·OIL

A LITTLE WILDROOT CREAM-OIL does a lot for your hair. Keeps your hair well groomed all day long. Leaves no trace of that greasy, plastered down look. Makes your hair look good and feel good.

JOHN FERGUS RYAN, AUTHOR OF *THE REDNECK BRIDE*, RESPONDS TO A REQUEST FOR HAIR INFORMATION

1. I used to know a Delta debutante who was fond of saying when vexed:

"I can't cope
With hair on the soap!"

2. I once met a traveling salesman who worked for Consolidated Fright Wigs of Waycross, Georgia.

3. Finally, a friend of mine in Knoxville said he attended the funeral there of a locally famous Negro transvestite who was known for his very long hair. The body was in the coffin, his hair arranged loosely around his head. When the undertaker brought down the lid, it caused a draft which drew the deceased's hair out of the coffin. The hair fell in a fringe around three sides of the end of the coffin where the dead man's head was. The lid was down and it had some sort of self-locking device that could not be opened without tools designed for the purpose. So, before the coffin was loaded into the hearse for the trip to the cemetery, the undertaker and one of his assistants drew straight razors from within the folds of their clothing and trimmed off the fringe of hair in front of the mourners.

CHAPTER THREE
GETTING FOLK BELIEFS BY THE SHORT HAIRS

According to *Brewer's Dictionary of Phrase and Fable*, "The fat of a dead red-haired person used to be in demand as an ingredient for poisons." It is a long-standing folk belief (which I do not share) that—just because Cain, as we all know, had a reddish-yellow beard and Judas had red hair—redheads are unreliable, deceitful and hot-tempered.

In Cornwall, England, the red-haired are believed to be unable to make good butter. I don't accept this for one instant.

In point of fact, a lot of people have been red-headed whom you don't think of as being red-headed. Woody Allen. Robert Penn Warren. Jane Fonda. Emily Dickinson. Mark Twain. Lizzie Borden. Martin Van Buren. General Custer (who had short hair for his last stand, by the way). George Bernard Shaw. Jill St. John. Let's just put it this way: it's hard to generalize.

We will get into Ronald Reagan later.

Okay. Hair standing on end. Hair does become more erect when adrenalin pumps; hence a prickling sensation. This is a poor copy of other animals' bristling or fanning out of crests or manes, which make them look larger, more formidable, less munchy. But Dr. Andrews, once of Beresford Chapel, Walworth, who attended a (non-electric) execution, was almost certainly talking through his hat when he said: "When the executioner put the cords on the criminal's wrists, his hair, though long and lanky, of a weak iron-gray, rose gradually and stood perfectly upright, and so remained for some time, and then fell gradually down again." This was in the nineteenth century, before television, when people would say all kinds of things.

Brushing your hair one hundred times before you go to bed, as mothers used to advise daughters to do, just wears your hair to a frazzle.

I'm sorry, but hair and nails do not continue to grow after death. What happens is that the flesh shrinks in so that they appear longer. I know there's a tale in some Eastern religion (Congregationalism?) about a tomb swinging open after fifty years and being *full of hair*, or at least I know someone told me such a tale, but I'm afraid it's the bunk. Charming, but the bunk.

My friend Vereen Bell had a friend (not me) who, in adolescence, shaved his chest so that it would be more hairy. This was a delusion. Shaving has no effect on hair growth. Since a shaved hair grows out blunt-ended and may be shorter, hence more erect, than it was before it was shaved, shaving will, to be sure, make a girl's legs or a boy's chest more prickly, at least for a while.

Bats, at least if you listen to students of bats, do not have the faintest inclination to tangle themselves in people's hair.
"I gave a woman a twenty-dollar bill to let me tangle a bat in her hair," a Dr. Tuttle has been quoted as saying in *The New Yorker*. "I put the bat in her hair, and twisted the hair

around and around, and then I let go, and out popped the bat, like a cork from underwater."

I don't know whether I would have wanted to see that or not. But if a woman will let a man put a bat in her hair for twenty dollars, then maybe my friend Nanette Crafton, who does hair, is right when she says, "Hairdressers know what men know: women are easy." Though you could have fooled me all these years.

A bat did get into the hair of my friend Sarah Gilbert, who has done hair in the past. She was a little girl when it happened. "I guess bats' wings are kind of pointy, but I thought it was teeth," she told me. "My mom got it out, but I don't know how."

"Maybe she used ice," I suggested.

"Ice?"

"You know, like you use ice to get gum out of kids' hair."

"That's an old wives' tale," she said. "Ice! Peanut butter! Ha! Ice will freeze the gum, but it'll freeze your hair, too, and break it. Use acetone. Which is found in most nail polish. But don't let it get on your scalp."

Peanut butter?

If you pluck a hair, nine more hairs will not "come to its funeral." Your body sprouts 200 new hairs a day and loses more or less the same number. Some days more, some days less. One hair does not care what goes on in the life of another.

Hair can't turn snow-white overnight. A shock to the system —fright, disease, offspring—can, like age, cause the hair to start taking on air bubbles instead of coloration: it may begin to grow out white, temporarily or from then on. What grows out white will stay white. But whatever hair was above the scalp before the shock won't change color. It may well be

true, as the writer Pete Dexter has maintained in a personal letter to me, that one of his golden retrievers "went stone white all over her head when we moved to the new house." But if that condition was evident as soon as they moved to the new house, then something must have shocked her earlier. That's how we scientists explain things.

In 1546, according to *Anomalies and Curiosities of Medicine* (published in 1896), a young man was thrown into prison for seducing his girl companion. When brought before the Emperor Charles V for judgment the following day, the seducer's "face was wan and pale and his hair and beard gray, the change having taken place in the night. His beard was filthy with drivel, and the Emperor, moved by his pitiful condition, pardoned him." Anybody who would seduce a girl companion and drivel in his beard would fake gray hair.

I have just looked Charles V up and learned that he was the Holy Roman Emperor who presided over the Diet of Worms. I would have called it something different, you would have called it something different, and I'll bet we would have instructed the boys in the lab to check that sumbitch's hair and beard for ashes or something.

The expression "the hair of the dog that bit you," referring to the belief that a drink will make inroads on a hangover, has been said to derive from a superstition that the best dog-bite antidote is burnt dog hair. A drink will make inroads on a hangover, if that is how you want to go through life. But the wisest course is to avoid getting drunk and hanging around with bad dogs.

Two French slang phrases for "to have a hangover" are *avoir mal aux cheveux*, "to have a hair-ache," and *avoir le cheveu triste*, "to have the sad hair." Drinking, especially in places where you might tumble into a vat of some "hair-care

product," does take a toll on your hair.

But that may be the price a student of hair has to pay. I'll say this: doing a book about hair has given me a good excuse to do one of my favorite things—drink and talk to women. For instance, I have all these napkins from somewhere, which contain a wealth of information about how women feel about their hair, which I can't read. Except for something about how Chris Evert's hairstyle and her game got more aggressive at the same time; and the same thing happened with Virginia Wade. And I believe I can reconstruct the following:

"I was at Kenneth's and Kenneth walked by and asked how I was coming. I said, 'Aldo's doing it hair by hair.'

" 'That won't take very long,' Kenneth said."

I never heard jokes like that before I started talking to women about hair.

THE VIRGIN MARY'S HAIR

"... was preserved at St. John Lateran and S. Maria sopra Minerva as well as in lesser churches throughout Rome; there was some in Venice, Bologna, Padua, Oviedo, Bruges, Assisi, St. Omar, Mâcon, in the Sante Chapelle in Paris, at Montserrat, and at St. Denis, in shades of gold to red to blonde to black and in quantities that would have made a grizzly bear look hirsute."

—Marina Warner, *Alone of All Her Sex*

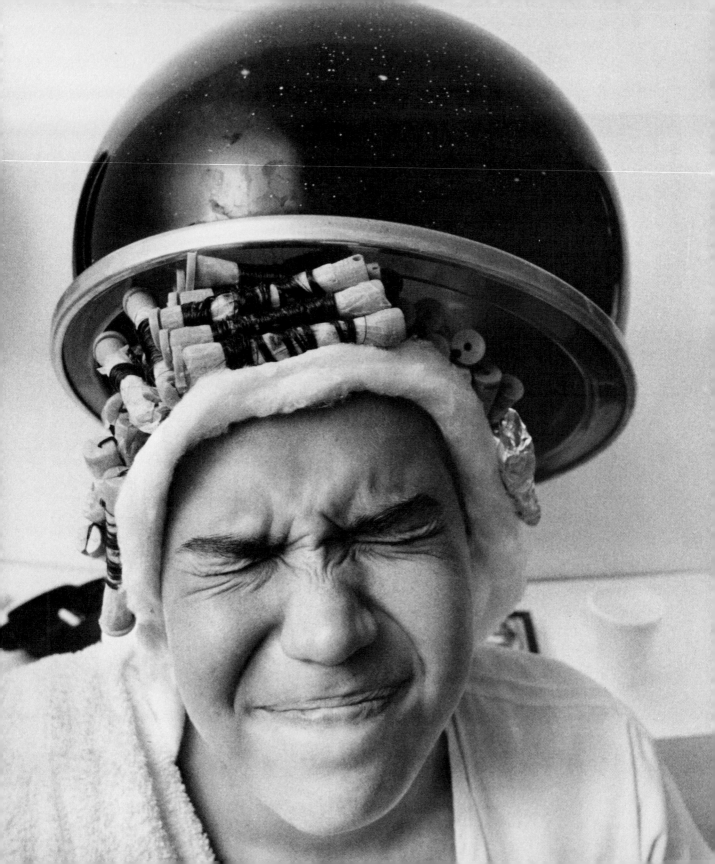

CHAPTER FOUR
TALKING TO WOMEN ABOUT THEIR HAIR

A number of women told me I was in over my head with this book. And I knew they were right.

I have never known how to say anything to women about their hair, except "Mmm." And that isn't always appropriate.

You could never tell my mother her hair looked nice, because she would never believe you. Or at least she would say she didn't believe you, and I believed her when she said it. What did I know? I figured there must be some sense in which I was lying or didn't know what I was talking about.

I now realize I should have said, "No, no, it *does* look nice. It..." It what? I would have had to learn hairdressers' terms.

All along, I felt my mother's hair was great stuff. Except when she came home from the beauty parlor. Then it looked tight and fake; you wanted to pull it off her head like a cap off an acorn; and she always went on about how she hated it. She would try to wash out what the beautician had done.

Another time I didn't like it was when she was giving herself a permanent, which smelled awful.

She would get so exasperated trying to get it just right for church. And then she would invariably bump it when she was getting in the car and mess it up. And get upset.

> **SOME NICE HAIR LINES—6**
>
> Fair tresses man's imperial race insnare, And beauty draws us with a single hair.
> —Alexander Pope, "The Rape of the Lock"

I wanted to say, "I think your hair is wonderful! I want you to be happy about it! Why let it bother you so much?"

But what did I know?

Working on this book, I would go into beauty salons, and see men fooling with women's hair for money and talking with them in certain tones.

And I would think, "Should I be here? Should this be going on?"

But somehow, when you're writing a book...

I asked women to talk about their hair, and many of them did.

Stephanie Salter:

"My hair has become physically addicted to mousse. Without mousse, it has no body and a mind of its own."

Esther Newberg:

"I'm just sitting here depressed that the hairdresser's not open on Monday so I can't go tell him to shave it all off.

"Especially when you're from a family in which everybody else has got thick hair that swings. It moves and has body. The kind of hair that people say, 'God, that's great hair.' Instead of it just lying there on top of your head.

"And there's something wrong with a part of your body that's affected by the humidity. My hair and my knees. I've got arthritis of the hair."

My sister Susan:

"When I was little my hair was so short Mother used to Scotch-tape a pink bow on my head so people would know I was a little girl. People had been saying, 'Sure is a cute little boy.' I was so big when this was going on I answered back to someone in the grocery store, 'I'm not a little boy, I'm a little girl.'

" 'How can you tell?' she asked.
"I said, 'Because I have on girl shoes.' "

Lois Betts:

"You know what he'll call your hair? The guy who's about to cut it? 'This.' He'll say, 'What are we going to do with *this*?' "

I don't remember who:

"Something about the frequency of babies crying makes your hair turn gray. It was in the *Times* or somewhere."

Harriett Davidson:

"Once they start putting those rollers in your hair, it's like this *pink environment.* You feel like you're being forced into it, but you want to do it because you want to be pretty."

Julie Marx:

"You want a hairdresser to say, 'This is *you!*' But they don't *know. You're* the only one who knows. You want to leave the hairdresser looking different, at last. But you don't want to leave not looking like yourself."

Marilyn Suzanne Miller:

"This is the most traumatic subject in a woman's life.

"I saw a woman on 'People's Court' with her hairdresser. She looked fine to me. She lost. Which is not the way we would all like to have it come out.

"I had it streaked in high school and all the streaked hairs fell out. And the real-color ones stayed in. So that was my punishment.

"Recently I decided to change my hairstyle, but I was so trepidatious about doing it that I found a hairdresser in L.A. who was willing to gradually cut my hair eight times, on eight separate occasions. Also willing to charge full price each time."

Lee Smith:
"There was this woman who told her hairdresser she was going to someone else. So he said, 'One last permanent for old times' sake.' Then he put the permanent fluid on and wouldn't put on the neutralizer until she succumbed to his wishes."

I don't remember who:
"You hear women saying, 'I'm going to Louis today'—they've got an appointment—'and I look terrible.' As if Louis gave a shit."

DREAM GIRLS of a DIM DECADE
SEVEN SUTHERLAND SISTERS
ENG. BY JOHN HELD JR. SINGER OF OLD SONGS

Janet Mansfield:
"When I was little I was fighting with my best friend, because she cheated me at a game we were playing, and I pulled out a fistful of her hair. We watched her hair blow away in the wind. And then we took off in opposite directions home."

My daughter Ennis and her friend Debbie Drucker:
"What I hate is soap opera hair. Helmet hair. Linda Evans —out on the side, nowhere connected to the head, pulled up and out. Looks stiff, doesn't move. That's important on 'Love Boat'—if the wind blows, it doesn't move the hair."

"If you're pregnant, had aspirin, have your period or have given blood in the last seventy-two hours, a permanent won't take."

"I was in the beauty parlor and a girl came in with, like,

pink splotches. She said, 'My friend gave me this and I've got to go to a wedding. I'd like it to be a little more magenta.'"

"After *10* came out I went to Jamaica and had my hair corn-rowed for ten dollars by a Jamaican lady. It took an hour on the beach, and it *hurt*, you know, like French braids? I sat there tearing. Every woman on the beach was like that. Then I got sunburned and my scalp peeled everywhere there was a part. I came home and went to Friendly's and nobody would sit across from me because they didn't want to look at me."

"On 'Dating Game,' every guy has a perm."

"In the sixties it was long straight hair, ironed on an ironing board, parted in the middle. Then everybody fooed it back like Farrah Fawcett, then everybody had a wedge like Dorothy Hamill, feathered on the side. 'Feathered,' that was big then."

"And wispies. Just cut a few bangs to come down over your forehead. Just a zit cover, actually."

"Now it's shag cuts, cut all over like Madonna. Her hair does not make sense, doesn't go together. You get a complete nice hairdo and then they take weird scissors and cut all over. You think they're cutting off all your hair."

"All the girls in the sororities have shoulder-length hair, cut every four weeks, takes an hour every morning. Beauty-contest hair. They must have to get up like five in the morning."

"I always used to cry every time I got a haircut. I wouldn't go to school the next morning. It's finished and I say, 'I like it.' Thinking, 'Sob.' The hairdresser goes, 'It looks excellent.' Your friend's sitting there waiting for you, looking like, 'Oh my God,' and saying, 'I like it.' You get out in the parking lot, 'I hate it, I hate it!' Can't even drive. Have a paranoid that everybody in the Chinese place is looking at you."

"People say, 'It makes you look older.' They say, 'I like it, I

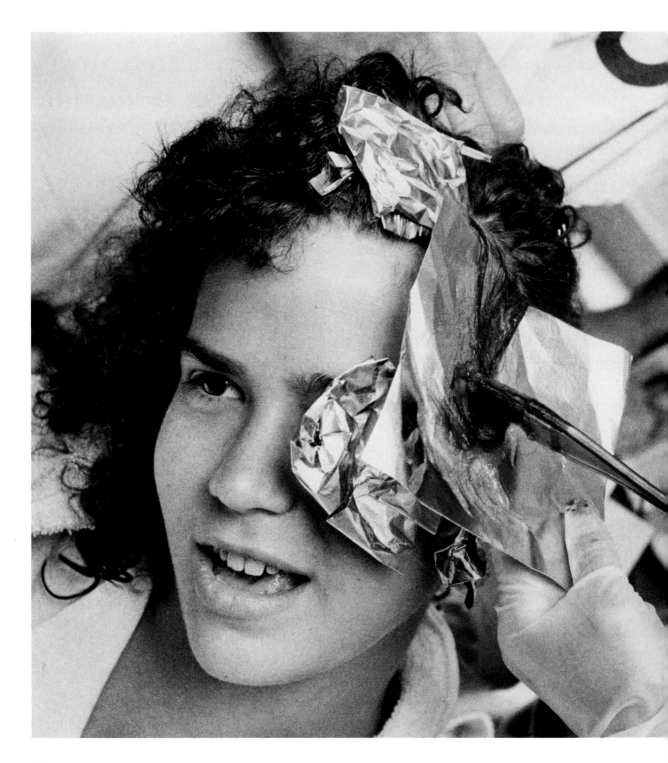

Bridget LeRoy has some color added.

really like it.' You know they're thinking, 'Oh my God.' You say, 'I'm not used to it yet. I'll look at it when it settles down.' You think it's never going to grow back."

"I used to make Princess Leia things—cover my ears with poufs of hair. People would say, 'You ought to be a hairdresser.' I'd think, 'Wouldn't that be cool?'"

"I remember hating washing my hair and then all of a sudden washing it morning, noon and night. When you're in the seventh or eighth grade you have to have your hair perfect."

Jan Yusk:

"My hair is so curly, especially when it's hot, I decided to get it straightened before we went to Europe. This sissy assistant was putting this gunk on me, the whole time saying, 'I hate to put this stuff on *anybody's* hair. This is *nasty* stuff.' And I was *sweating*. He pulled some of it out this way to the front, some of it out this way to the back, some out this way to the side. And when it dried it was still that way. Sticking out. And I mean it was like Dagwood all over. He kept trying and trying to comb it out and pretty soon *he* was sweating.

"Keith came up and said, 'You've always been better at blow-drying your hair than I am. Go home and see what you can do.'

"I came home, tried to change it, and it just all . . . stuck . . . straight . . . out. I called him and said, 'Keith, not only can I not leave the country like this, I can't leave the bathroom. I'm afraid for the dog to see me like this.'

"So I went back and he cut it all off. And I came home and lay on the bed and cried. Jack tried to comfort me. I told him, 'It's like I lost a part of my body.'

"I had to go all through Europe with my head in a hat.

"I kept going back to Keith. He was the only one who could cut my hair right."

A LOOSENING UP...
Evolution of the Hairdo in Hair-dye Ads, 1956–1980

1956

1963

Elaine Wood:

"It's security, it's trademark, it's something to hide behind, it's image, it's identity.

"Even when I'm feeling really confident, I'm still insecure about my hair. My hair's the last thing. I still want to check it out.

"I described my hair as always being nondescript. I wanted one of those hairdos that would never get me in trouble. Nobody would ever say anything about it. Then I went to Girard Bolais in New York, after I got back from Paris. I got this crazy asymmetrical haircut, no hair on one side and a big mess on the other; that haircut was so fine.

"I got tired of it after three weeks, but I decided I always want to keep changing.

Hate that gray? Wash it away!

Now! Color only the gray

without changing your natural hair color!

Loving Care Hair Color Lotion by CLAIROL

1965

Introducing
"Blondest Blonde"
New Miss Clairol 12
It's the lightest of all.

CLAIROL

Wait till you see what we do for you next.

1974

"I admire girls who come in one day all white, the next day a green streak, the next day purple spikes. A spirit behind it of total abandon."

I forget who:
"Your hair will turn on you. What's beautiful at thirty, at fifty looks like you're trying to pretend you're young."

I forget who:
"I had my head back in the basin having some color put in and I heard people saying, 'It's *smoking*!'

"And I started to look up and somebody threw water on my head and somebody else yelled, 'It's smoking *worse*!'

"Freon was leaking out of the air conditioner and reacting

1975

1977

with the peroxide on my hair, and the water made it react more.

"I didn't pay for it."

Sarah Rockwell:

"I went into this place on Newbury Street where all the women from my old high school had been turned into fabulous beauties. I was feeling really drab. I said, 'Fix me up.'

"'What do you really want?' he said.

"I said, 'I don't know, I guess the way it's always been, just parted down the middle and hanging there.'

"I wound up getting this *perm*. The most vile-smelling experience you ever had in your life. I had to write a check for seventy-five dollars and then hide it from my husband.

1980

1980

...AND TIGHTENING BACK?

"And you really don't look all that different. And if you do, you spend time in the bathroom rinsing it all out.

"You're tempted by the image of Pamela Ewing on 'Dallas' —but you can't look like that. They have fans blowing at them and things.

"Most hair really conforms to gravity."

I never knew what to say to any of these women in reply. Because I had not yet developed the Hair Theory of Human Evolution.

I'll tell you what I like. I like it when women blow straight upward from their lower lip, when they're not-uncheerfully tired, so that their hair is ruffled, lifted, slightly.

ROMANTIC HAIR GESTURES AMONG THE LITERATI

I GEORGE SAND AND ALFRED DE MUSSET

He told her it was all over between them. She went home and cut off her long black hair. Then she went out and bought a skull. In it she placed her hair and the only letter of his she had left. For a while she kept all this near her bed. According to one account, writes Curtis Cate, she then had the hair "delivered in a parcel to Alfred, who happened to be entertaining guests in his room. He half opened the package, then hastily thrust it into a drawer. His friends, realizing that something was weighing on his mind, soon withdrew. Opening the drawer, Alfred undid the package with a beating heart, ran his hands through the locks he had so often stroked, then buried his face in them with a groan."

According to another account, Sand went to Musset's townhouse in person. When he opened the door, she sank to her knees, holding the skull in her outstretched hands. Silently she went to Alfred on her knees, and touched him with the skull. He knocked it to the floor, and from it a long black tress emerged. Alfred did not speak, but escorted Sand out. He returned to the skull. Kicked it to one side. Bent down and picked up the locks. "Buried his burning forehead in them with frenzy."

II DANTE GABRIEL ROSSETTI

When his wife, Eleanor Siddal, died, he buried a sheaf of his poems in manuscript—the only copy—between her hair and cheek.

Later he reconsidered, and had the poems exhumed and published.

A WOMAN FRIEND OF MINE, WHO SHALL REMAIN NAMELESS, TELLS OF HAVING LUNCH WITH A WOMAN FRIEND OF HERS, WHOM WE SHALL CALL H.

"She said, 'Your hair looks good.'

"Which it didn't. 'No it doesn't,' I said.

"Then _____ _____ stopped by the table and H. told her, 'Your hair looks good.'

"'No it doesn't,' she said. 'It needs to be cut.'

"Then _____ _____ walked by with her bright red hair and H. said, 'Oh, _____, I like the color of your hair.'

"Then somebody, _____ _____ or a guy like that, who's got just little wisps of hair on the sides, walks by and H. says to him, 'Oh, are you losing your hair?'

"I said to her, 'What is this, are you obsessed?' She said she's found that when she's nervous, all she can think to talk about is hair. The other day, she caught herself about to tell someone her hair looked nice on the phone."

IT'S THE LITTLE THINGS

Vanessa Williams, the first black Miss America, was the only black child in her school when she was six. Other children asked to feel her hair, but she wouldn't let them. When she was in the sixth grade, she secretly wished she looked like Blythe, in the seventh, who "had a part in the middle of this straight, platinum-blonde hair. She typified what the American WASP should look like. You know, she put her hair behind her ears."

CHAPTER FIVE
CUTTERS AND SHAPERS
KENNETH

Futurists have suggested— *seriously*—that the haircutter on the horizon is a tiny, nestling, computerized robot that stays in your hair all the time and is programmed to keep it constantly at the desired length.

Oh yeah? That would eliminate a mythic figure: the person who takes your head and the immediate future of your personality into his or her hands and knows your anxieties and listens to you talk.

No robot is going to displace Kenneth. His salon just off Fifth Avenue in Manhattan is modeled after the "great beauty houses" he used to see in the movies. "Russian wolfhounds. People in the middle of the day in evening gowns. Complete fantasy." In reality, silk wallpaper; lots of chintz; sleek gray and black Formica surfaces; mirrors, mirrors, mirrors. "I always see the client in the mirror. I never see myself. Like Dracula."

When he decided, growing up in Syracuse forty years ago, to become a hairdresser, "I was shunned by my high school fraternity. Any male hairdresser was suspected of doing all kinds of things to little boys, little girls, chickens and dogs and cats."

No one has shunned Kenneth lately, certainly not since Jacqueline Kennedy brought him to the Camelot White House. "It could have been George or François or Vidal," he says today. "It happened to be Kenneth. And that's all I have to say about Mrs. Onassis." Who is, of course, still a client.

The first place he worked was the Starlet Beauty Bar. He turned it into *the* place in Syracuse. Now his clientele are the very rich and tasteful: "people who live with their hair on a level other than that of current fad and fashion."

But in some ways, the business is the same. "I don't mind saying we do four million dollars a year here, but it all comes down to someone looking in the mirror before you do something, and then after, and they are happy. It comes down to being a very good servant, and that doesn't bother me.

"People I've had failures with are people who don't know how to treat the servants."

LOUIS LICARI

Louis Licari is widely regarded as New York's state-of-the-art colorist. He runs the color floor at La Coupe, where a woman may spend four and a half hours and $225 to have her grayness or mousiness altered—camouflaged, rehighlighted—subtly, so it blends, it adapts, it doesn't leap out again from the roots when the camouflage is growing out.

The hair's natural, not-to-be-borne-any-longer pigmentation is removed by carefully timed chemical soaks, then livelier tones are soaked in strategically.

"I started out as a painter," says Licari. "It's a built-in advantage."

Is hair coloring like painting, then?

"No," says Licari. "One is an art and one is a skill: you can learn to color hair."

But tell his clients that. The brunette locks of Bridget LeRoy, 21, aren't graying, but she wants them touched up with strokes of red and yellow.

"As long as it's like desert colors," she says. "I want to be in tune with the coyote. I want to look like I'm painted. I want to look like a Georgia O'Keeffe."

"The yellow," says one of Licari's staff of colorists, "is going to have a tangerine quality."

"That really confuses me," says Bridget. But she knows she's in good hands.

VITTORIO

Vittorio Di Silvestro works in the salon at Saks Fifth Avenue. "Women are apt to be more personal with their hairdresser than with their doctors, their gynecologist or even their psychiatrist.

"Professional women come in who've been with stuffy bankers, stuffy lawyers, all day long. I'm very earthy. They can relax. If they're still feeling stuffy, I'll bring them down to the person they are, the person they want to be.

"Some women you got to be more of a gentleman with, others more raunchy. But I'm being a gentleman while I'm being raunchy. I grew up in the streets of the South Bronx. I wanted to be an actor. But this is kind of a stage.

"I'll do four roommates, each talking about the others. They're trying to get something out of me. I'm cool. Keep my mouth shut.

"Out of twenty-five male hairdressers, maybe three of them are straight. The other ones say, 'C'mon.' To gay people, the whole world is gay. They think the Pope is gay.

"I love women. I'm a womanizer. If you do an average of fifty women a week, law of averages, one of them is going to hit on you. I enjoy doing men's hair, but if you told me I couldn't do men for the rest of my life it wouldn't bother me. If you said I couldn't do women, you'd have to put a gun to my head."

85

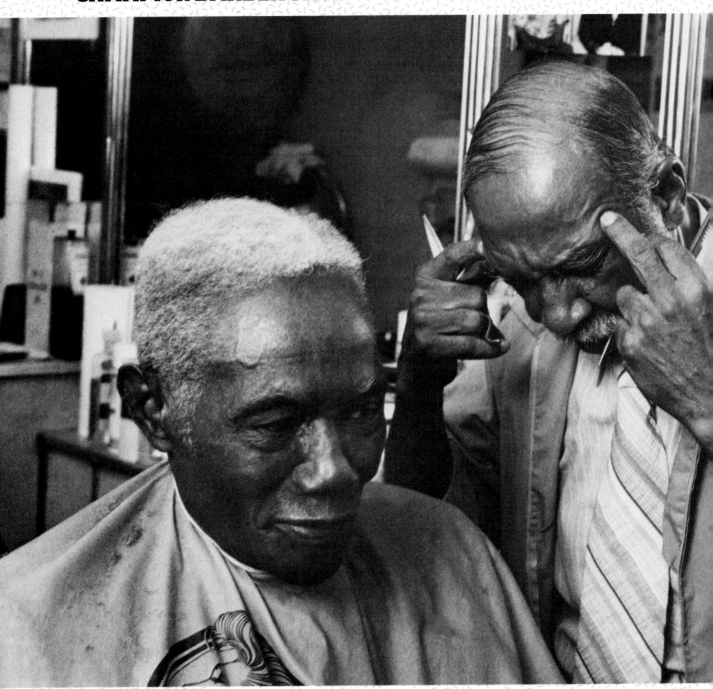

"Barber's got to live as careful a life as a minister," says Moses Jenkins of the Champion Barber Shop in Harlem, where a haircut starts at four dollars. "Just like these athletes—a lot is expected out of certain people. And a barber falls into that category. A barber can't be just jumping up and down doing anything he wants to do just any kind of way. Barbering's just like a church. From a drunkard to the pastor comes in."

And testifies. Old customer Bruce Johnson tells about the time in 1929 when he was fourteen, living in Miami, and a white man cheated him out of $1.75, giving change. Johnson demanded his money, and the man hit him hard in the face. "People yelling at me, 'Don't fight him, don't fight him, you know you going to get lynched.'

"I started running across the golf links and heard that man yelling, 'Get him, get him,' and you know they were lynching people then. I ran and ran and jumped in a truck head first. And you know I was lucky enough, that truck took me one block from my house.

"'Don't go in your house!'

people said. I hid, and the next morning my mouth was swelled to where I couldn't open it enough to get a flapjack in. Somebody took me to Palm Beach, Florida. Where you think I wound up at? From Miami to Palm Beach to Jacksonville to New York.

"I waited three years till 1932 and went back home. And who you think I see? He said, 'Oh my God I'm gonna kill you.' I caught a bus that night back to New York.

"You know what time I went back next? Nineteen forty-five. Waited thirteen more years. I'd been in the Army, got my uniform on. I went back to declare myself. I quit running. I done fought a war for Uncle Sam. If I'm gonna die now, I die for myself. And I told my brother, 'I'm gonna kill him now. Don't care anything now.'

"And my brother said, 'You know, I see the boy every day. He married and everything.'

"And I go in the shoestore. He in the shoestore. I say, 'Hey, Jimmy.'

"And he say, 'Hey, Bruce.'

"He know me.

"Put his hand out like this. Said 'I'm married and got

kids. Whatever I did, I was young then.'

"I said, 'I'm glad you feel that way.'

"He got two kids, he showed me a picture of 'em out of his wallet.

"I was thirty years old. Been away from home since fourteen. But we got to be all right. Got to be good friends. It was all right."

"Raise a haircut fifty cents up here and people squawk," says Jenkins. "Downtown, cost you fifty dollars."

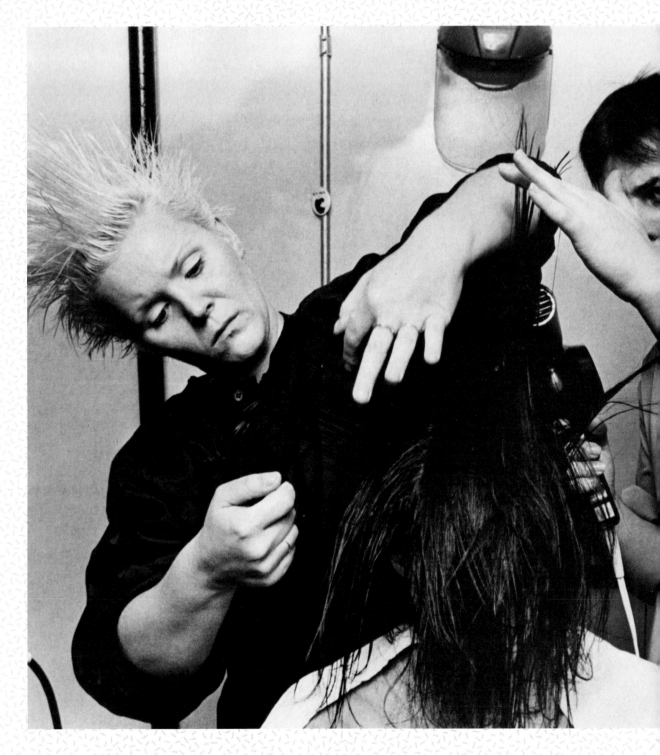

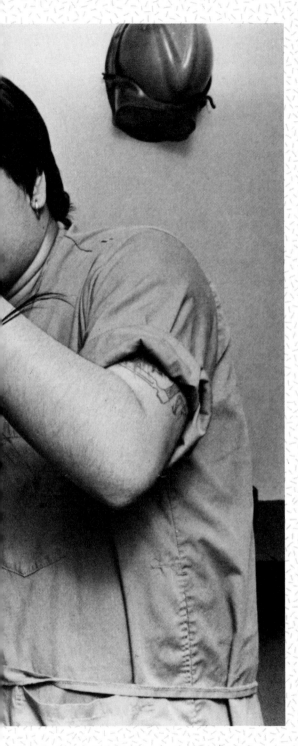

INDUSTRIAL HAIR

Why does Diane Ries call her East Village shop Industrial Hair?

"I depend on the steel industry for my shears, the chemical industry for my shampoo, the fabric industry for my towels—and if we understand that hair itself is a fabric, we can color it, bleach it, starch it.

"If something's natural it'll rot. Whoever said natural is healthy was wrong. Beauty and health don't belong on the same page in a magazine. There's nothing healthy about beauty.

"If we want hair to be responsive, we have to do a certain amount of controlled damage with technical prowess so it achieves a certain reasonable response."

And why does she have handcuffs and shackles hanging from the ceilings?

"That's for people who touch their hair while I'm working on it. They want to touch it. They want to put their glasses on and look. That's why surgeons use anesthesia.

"People come in here and say, 'You can do anything you want, but don't let my ears show'—I don't know what it is about people and ears, they're afraid of their ears—'and leave it long in back and don't layer it, but you can do anything you want.' I say, 'Well there's the door, why don't you leave?'

"I do not rent my hands. There is a romance in my hands. The momentum that builds as I work—that's what other stylists don't have.

"The stylist is a master, there's no doubt about that. The question is whether he's a kind one or a cruel one."

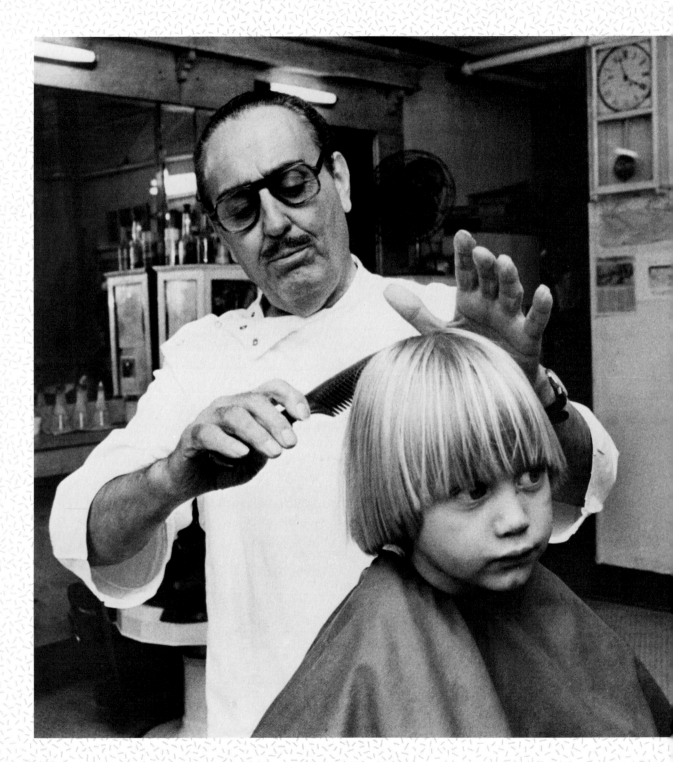

MR. KAY

Kay Demetriou—Mr. Kay —started out, as a boy in England, sweeping the floors of an exclusive shop. At eleven he was a lather boy, and at twelve he was already cutting. He was so short he had to stand on a box. He noticed the shop's proprietor standing behind him. "You don't trust me?" the boy asked. "I'm *learning* from you," said the old hand.

Now Mr. Kay owns, at Broadway and 104th Street, what he calls "the only original classic barbershop left in New York City. Been in continuous operation since 1907. To set up a shop like this today would cost you half a million dollars." Carrera marble fixtures. Pressed-metal ceiling. Sterling silver vessels for tonics and witch hazel. And, outside, a pole with a story behind it.

One day in 1983, Mr. Kay heard a shot, ran next door and found his neighbor dead. "This is terrible. He's a human being, he's not a fly. I wanted to get close to him, talk to him. No answer. I bent down to kiss him on the forehead. I began to cry; not from fear, from sadness.

I didn't see anybody who did the shooting, but these guys, in order to silence me, apparently, chopped my pole.

"But this new one is a six-footer. Only one left in Manhattan. The others are short. You know who loved the pole? The Japanese. They did a documentary a few days ago, and went crazy for the pole.

"I'm always challenging so-called hairstylists—challenging them on television —to do a crewcut or a flat-top. They're supposed to be stylists. It's a *style*, right? A crewcut you have to look in the mirror and cut, don't look at the hair. They can't do that. They don't have the training."

HAIR SHOW

If you think you love a parade, if you think you want to run away and join a circus, then you ought to see a hair show.

Man up there doing a foxy woman's hair in a choreographic way to the sound of "What's Love Got to Do With It"—meanwhile espousing hair products, explicating haircutting theory and evangelizing for the hair-care industry in general.

"You know by the sound of my voice I bring a message. It's just a thing I was given. I can teach. I can teach. Four lines in the cranium, four lines in the entire world!

"If you see hair comin' out in your comb, it's time to take Rejuvenation home!

"You young ladies look so *good* on stage. It just makes me feel *so* good. Without the ladies, the men can't make it. And without God, nothing is possible.

"Big D! The relaxer of the 80s.

"It takes blacks working with whites to make green. And that's the only thing that means any*theen.*

"This man here is the fastest rat-tail comb in the west. When he came to us he couldn't talk. Couldn't walk. Couldn't breathe. Had prob-

lems with his belief. And now —speak some French for these people!"

And that's just in the afternoon. In the evening surreal poufs and tendrils, borne aloft by models who move like sylphs, who trained under jaguars, go head to head to held-high head until, along about one a.m., the winning stylist's inspiration has profited him, what? A trophy? What do you think this is, a small operation? No. He comes away with a Rolls Royce.

Most people who aspire to do hair go to beauty school now. There aren't many barber colleges left. But Leo Galletta's in New York is one.

BEAUTY SCHOOL

(Part of a longer work by Sarah Gilbert)
I can't quite remember the reason why I decided to go to Beauty School except that maybe I was too short to be a model and not bright enough to be a stewardess. There were just no requirements for being a beautician. Anyhow, the sign on the door read Celebrity School of Beauty, where inside a shampoo and set cost three-fifty and for fifty cents more you could get a blue rinse. This attracted the State Hospital crowd down

the road and on Saturday mornings they would pile into a green van and come on over.

Since my first day started on a Saturday, my first customer was Mrs. Foster, a sweet grandmotherly type, who promptly sat down at my station and started hissing at me. I was scared. But not as scared as I was when she removed her teeth and started screaming.

That same week a perfectly sane suburban housewife sat down at my station for a cut and color. She asked me to mix her hair color with pig's urine, which she had brought with her in a neat little Maxwell House jar—she said it was a natural process that the Greeks used to use. Well, I didn't know about that, but I did know that Mrs. Foster wasn't the only loony I was going to have to do in my career. I also got the leapers and the jumpers, who would get out of my chair and start running. Sometimes a patron dies on you. That's really bad.

It doesn't take long before a student begins to realize that what can be done for other women's hair can be done for her too. She walks into the school that first day with virgin hair, and walks out with something entirely different. All of a sudden she really looks like a beautician. It starts off slowly at first with just a short trim here or there, then picks up speed. Spunsand, bashful blonde, winsome wheat, frivolous fawn rest comfortably atop thermal waves, heat waves, cold waves. The girls are rolled on blue rods, pink rods, pink and gray rods and with piggy-backing for long hair and spiral curls for short. No longer are these the drab girls that didn't make high-school cheerleading, but glamourous women in a new world.

Once I did a chemical job on a woman who had four different colors of hair. Coming from her scalp was a grayish-brown color which ran into a bluish-black color that melted into a wheat color and eventually settled on a dull black color for the ends. I'd never quite seen hair that color before but I knew one thing—it wasn't natural. She wanted a perm and I asked her the first question any trained beauty operator is supposed to ask a new perm customer, "Ma'am, do you have any color on your hair?" And she said, "No." Well, I knew better and got a perm for color-treated hair and after I rolled her on small blue rods, I applied the solution. Within minutes those rods started smoking and falling off her head—*with* the hair still attached. It was scary but not as scary as looking at her was. She was smiling. It wasn't bothering her at all. I rinsed her and got the rest of those rods out of her hair and fast—but it was no use. Her head was full of big bald patches. "It happens all the time, honey. Don't you worry about it," she said. She wore a lime green halter top and leopard pedal pushers and her lipstick was all over her mouth and she just kept right on smiling as I tried in vain to fix her hair. She was just an American consumer who had tried Lady Grecian Formula—a highly combustible product when mixed with a perm. She was lucky she didn't go up in flames. When I told her this she just said, "But I like it." Another thing about beauty school—there are just no requirements for being a patron either.

The last time I visited Celebrity's everything was the same. In this day of blow dryers and curling irons, Celebrity's was sitll giving shampoos and sets. The posters that had been on the walls since the 1950s were still hanging, displaying beautiful women, with beautiful smiles and beautiful beehives. Miss Peggy said the crazies still came in on Saturdays and that a couple of them still asked about me.

As I stood there I saw a lady trying to tear something out of a magazine slowly so no one could see her. She kept the magazine closed. Looking around with the hand inside the cover, she tore slowly, slowly, a little bit at a time, looking around all the time. Once in a while it's recipes but most of the time it's hairdos.

IN 1906, "WAHOO SAM" CRAWFORD, THE DISTINGUISHED DETROIT TIGER, IS INTERVIEWED BY *THE SPORTING NEWS* ABOUT THE BARBERSHOP HE RAN IN WAHOO, NEBRASKA, BEFORE BECOMING A BALLPLAYER

"Did you go in for art treasures with which to soothe the weary eyelid?"

"The walls of the room reeked with standard masterpieces, and people came miles to see them. Among my treasures was a massive canvas direct from the Hoffman House Salon on Broadway. Perhaps you have seen copies of the original, which I owned. The celebrated painting depicted a group of the nation's leading men."

"Can you name them, Mr. Crawford?"

"Well, yes. Inspector Byrnes was there in a policeman's cap; Chauncey Depew and his side whiskers; Buffalo Bill in a fur-trimmed overcoat; Nat Goodwin, the actor; August Belmont, in a plug hat; Grover Cleveland, with his face hanging over his collar; Billy Edwards, the prize fighter; General Miles and Davis R. Hill, who needed a bottle of hair restorer, were among those present. Everybody smoked a cigar of the same brand, the name of which was printed on a red cinch worn by the cigar.

"Then there was another on a background of green, with plenty of smoke—the Robert E. Lee and the Natchez racing on the Mississippi. A most spirited work of art.

"Besides these art treasures, there was an ornate glass-front cabinet of richly carved pine, containing private microbe mugs with the gents' names in gilt letters on each mug. And I forget just how many cuspidors I did have."

TAKING YOUR HAIR INTO YOUR OWN HANDS

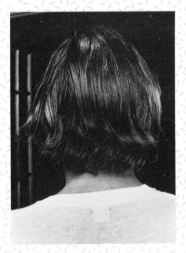

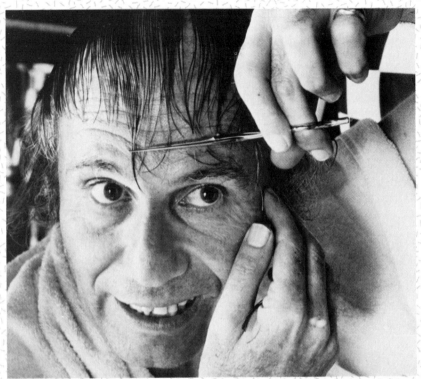

Twelve years ago, publisher Don Hutter figured out how to cut his hair, and he hasn't looked back since. Or, rather . . . "My big breakthrough," Hutter says, "was when I turned my back to the main mirror, and held the small mirror in front of me. That way, you're cutting actual left and actual right." In trying to get an actual grip on this concept, I have myself gone into the bathroom, turned around and around and around, and fallen down. "I have very straight hair," says Hutter. "It's pretty easy to do."

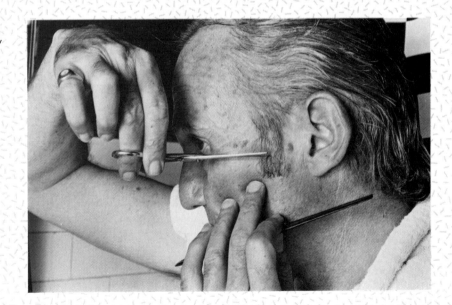

CHAPTER SIX
SHAMPOO AND OTHER GUNK

Sebum. Our enemy? Our friend?

That is a deep question. How deep, I had no idea until I began to look into hair.

Sebum. What is it?

A small country somewhere whose emperor has outraged our red-haired President?

No. It is the grease that our skin's sebaceous glands, which usually grow attached to hair follicles, give off. What does sebum do? According to the *Encyclopedia Britannica*:

> This semiliquid mixture of bizarre fatty acids, triglycerides, waxes, cholesterol, and cellular detritus does not emulsify readily, is toxic to living tissues, and seems to serve little purpose except as an emollient.

Except as an emollient, is it? Perhaps the *Encyclopedia Britannica* has never needed an emollient real bad. Chapstick and calamine lotion are emollients. My dog Mollie does hardly anything that I *need* her to do except mollify. And why did the *Britannica* feel that "bizarre" was necessary?

"Some investigators," the *Britannica* goes on to say, "have dismissed sebum as a useless substance and sebaceous glands as archaic organs that do greater harm than good."

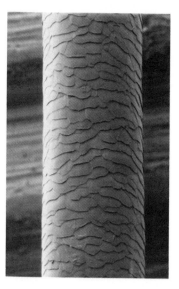

Clean hair.

Dirty hair.

HAIR TESTING

In Clairol's labs, hair is gone through with everything from a fine-tooth combing machine to an electron microscope. The latter will magnify a hair up to 300,000 times, if the hair is coated—conditioned—with a few Angstroms of gold, for conductivity. (Electrons flow into hair but not through it, which is why your hair stands on end when you use shampoo or grab a live wire.)

Someone is breaking down cuttlefish ink in man's tireless but so far fruitless quest to synthesize natural pigment (melanin). In the Constant Humidity Room people test luster, which is measured mathematically in terms of how much light (candelas-per-square-meter) a hair reflects.

Most of the swatches and tresses are European, from DeMeao Brothers in New York, but from time to time a researcher's lock comes in handy. "We're guinea pigs more than twice a month around here," says one employee. "For *lots* of things." There is also a head, with human hair rooted in a plastic scalp, whose name is Kay. "I used to take her for a ride in the car," says a researcher. "Take her to the bank with me. Just to get environmental testing. We'd have more fun." But Kay doesn't get out much lately, and you can see it in her eyes.

Dismissed sebum, have they? As easy as that. I'd like to see those investigators' hair.

Sebum is implicated in acne and smegma, but those are not concerns of this book. Sebum makes hair oily—too oily, for most contemporary tastes—and catches environmental dirt.

We ought not to get too high and mighty about sebum. Hair itself is a waste product—dead cells that the skin is pushing out. Did it ever occur to any of these investigators that sebum might lubricate these cells in their passage? Maybe without sebum, hair would be so "clean" that as it grew it would squeak. Once when Peter Davison, the poet and editor, asked Howard Nemerov, the poet, what he was doing on Cape Cod, Nemerov replied: "Listening to my hair grow." That's for poets. I don't want to hear mine.

Sebum, though bad for adolescent pores, is good for hair. Ask any hair professional. Many of them will tell you they wash their own hair once a month or even less frequently; rinsing is enough for them. Christiaan, the New York hairstylist, has not washed his hair in eight years, and he has convinced many of his friends among the fashion avant-garde (according to the New York *Post*) to follow his example.

American hair is useless to wigmakers, because it has been so dried out, coated and generally denatured by shampoos, conditioners, sprays, permanent lotions, mousses and so on. (There's your "bizarre.") The best material for human-hair wigs is what comes out in the brushes of Sicilian women whose only hair treatments are rinsing and a little olive oil. They save their brushings, and periodically a hair dealer comes around and buys them. Used to trade them pots and pans, but lately they're getting wise.

When I learned all this, I went for four days without doing anything to my hair besides rinsing it in the shower and combing it. And it looked like I had been using it to clean carburetors

with. Perhaps what it comes down to is that if my hair doesn't
have an element of, well, fluff . . . I mean offhand fluff. I don't
mean anything you would think of as fluff. I mean, I don't
make any effort to fluff it, but if I shampoo it and condition it
and comb it and let it dry . . . Sometimes. I hate talking about this.

When I was a boy, I thought that if my hair would only look
like that of Dr. Rex Morgan in the comic strip, I would be
happy with it. I wanted it to lie down, in this kind of smooth
and solid way, slightly elevated in the front, but with the eleva-
tion merging seamlessly into the rest. I wanted my hair to lie
right! Odd concept: to lie right.

This was back in the early fifties, when the hair-care scene
was not as we know it today. All the shampoo ads seemed to
be for women. Every now and then, with reluctance because I
associated hair-washing with burning eyes, I would wash my
hair with bar soap when I took a bath. My mother would
recommend that I put some vinegar on it, but I didn't want to
be taking any recommendations in the bathroom, and anyway: *vinegar?* I would dry my hair, more or less, and put a
little Vitalis on it. And try to plaster down the general rumpled-
ness (if there was anything I shrank from it was the wet-wavy
look) and then to roach the front part back, give it a little
pompadour. Well, you wouldn't *call* it a pompadour.

And it looked awful. I looked awful. And judging from photographs, I didn't even realize how awful I looked.

I would roach it some more. Sometimes it would look sort
of like Mickey Rourke's does today, only much shorter. It would
separate, like bad milk. I wanted a little lift! A little theme! A
little shape! I wanted somehow to regularize my face, which
was odd, spotty, asymmetrical, lumpily squarish. I felt that hair
should look like it is at least willing, if not inclined, to be where
it is; but I wanted it to be where I wanted it to be, which I was
not very clear about.

105

I still don't know how Dr. Rex Morgan gets his hair to do like it does. But he has long since ceased to be my role model. (Let's face it, he is never going to develop an interest in women.) I secretly wish my hair looked like Robert Redford's. Like it just happened to fall the way hair ought to fall. But if it did, it probably wouldn't go with me.

What I want, I now realize, is what everyone wants: body. Volume. Not the kind of volume it sometimes gets, when it looks like it belongs on the head of a far larger person. I mean just sort of casual volume. So my head would look different. Like the head of a normal person who doesn't take a great deal of trouble about his appearance but who is just the sort of person whose hair is neither lank nor whorly but naturally fullish in the right places. That's all I ask.

And the only way I have been able to come close to that effect is by shampooing and conditioning, every day, except for those days when I never take my cap off. Since hair products is a $38.2 billion industry, I must not be alone.

(I made that figure up. As I was doing my research, I kept thinking I would be able to piece together such a figure, but who knows what a figure like that means anyway? Let us just say that more money is spent in this country on hair than is spent in, say, Asia on everything. If that is not true, I think it is close enough to the truth to give us something to think about.)

True shampoo has been around for only about forty years. The word *shampoo* was brought into the English language shortly before the eighteenth century, by Anglo-Indians who adapted it from the Hindi *campo*, which means "knead." For more than a hundred and fifty years, *shampoo* (sometimes spelled *champoe*) had nothing to do with hair. It meant "massage." From the *Oxford English Dictionary*, here are some usages in that sense that you might enjoy:

"Had I not seen several China merchants shampooed before me, I should have been apprehensive of danger."

"She [an Indian wife] first champoes her husband, and fans him to repose; she then champoes the horse."

"In Tahiti, too, a traveller, on entering a house, is always given a mat to lie on, and his weary limbs are shampooed while food is prepared." (This from Charles Dickens, 1898.)

Somewhere around the mid-nineteenth century the word began to be used in reference to rubbing and washing the head, and then to the cleansing agent used. That agent, however, was some form of soap—which leaves an insoluble, sheen-dulling fatty scum, like a bathtub ring. It takes vinegar or lemon juice to rinse that residue out.

It was not until after World War II, when great advances were made in all forms of detergents, that true shampoo came in. (Though an early form of one had been invented in the thirties.) One end of a detergent molecule combines with water, the other adheres to dreck. When the water is rinsed out, away goes all the dreck and all the detergent. The first mass-market shampoos were Halo and Prell. (I have heard women run Prell down, but it is the only shampoo brand that has remained steadily popular over the years.)

Since they touch the skin and some people are allergic to certain ingredients, everything in hair products has to appear on the package. Ingredients must be listed in order, according to how great a percentage of the product each represents. The bulkiest item comes first, and so on down. Except that any ingredient whose volume is no greater than .1 percent of the whole may be listed in any order with all other such ingredients. The great majority of ingredients fall into this category. So even though Red Clover Extract may be fourth on the whole list of ingredients, and FD&C Red #4 may be thirty-fifth, the latter may be .1 percent of the volume and the former .001 percent.

Let's take, just at random, Swiss Formula St. Ives Aloe Vera Shampoo with Vitamin E.

Ingredient number one is water. Fair enough. The same is true of the human body.

Ingredient number two is Sodium Laureth Sulfate. This is by far the most important ingredient. It is the surfactant. It is what makes this product a detergent, therefore a shampoo. It gloms onto the dirt. Other popular surfactants are Sodium Lauryl Sulfate and Ammonium Laureth Sulfate.

Ingredients number three and four are Cocamide DEA and Cocamidoprophyl Betaine. These are derived from coconut oil. They stabilize the shampoo's foam. A shampoo's thick sudsy lather provides no benefit other than giving you a sense that you are getting something for your money. (Suds are like ideal hair: curly, organized, nice to the touch.) These coca things also provide viscosity, which gives you the same bene-fit. (Who wants a runny shampoo?) A cheaper thickening agent is sodium chloride, but since people have started looking at ingredients and recognizing sodium chloride as nothing but table salt, sodium chloride is out of favor.

The other ingredients are as follows:

Aloe Vera Gel
Tocopherol Acetate (E)
Watercress Extract
White Nettle Extract
Glycerol PABA
Sage Extract
Rosemary Extract
Chamomile Extract
Citric Acid
Hydrolized Milk Protein
Panthenol
Retinyl Palmitate (A)
Ergocalciferol (D)
Methylparaben
Fragrance
Sodium Chloride (just a dash)
Quaternium-15
FD&C Yellow #5
FD&C Blue #1

All these ingredients probably fall into the .1-percent-or-less category. Almost all of them are of highly marginal significance, except in marketing.

Aloe vera may condition the hair to a certain extent (we will come to that when we come to conditioner).

The items with (E), (A) and (D) after them contain those vitamins. But since vitamins cost $250 a pound in bulk you are not going to find more than eentsy smidgins of them in shampoo, and at any rate vitamins applied to the outside of hair have no demonstrable effect.

All those herbal extracts may add a bit to the fragrance, and they look good in the fine print.

PABA is Para Amino Benzoic Acid, sometimes referred to as a sunscreen. What PABA does is to provide a bit of a coating that somewhat ameliorates sun damage to the hair cuticle.

Citric Acid counteracts shampoo's generally alkaline effect, which may cause hair to look dull.

Let us assume that the Milk Protein is milk protein. Chemists who break down shampoos for companies creating cheaper knockoff versions sometimes find no trace of lactation in shampoos heralding milk. At any rate, milk protein is like other proteins in shampoo: it adds some conditioning, as we will see.

Panthenol is a new, very expensive item, which is actually vitamin H. It can help tighten the follicle, therefore holding the hair in somewhat longer before it yields to its natural fate and drops out.

Methylparaben is important, because it keeps bacteria from growing in the shampoo (so does formaldehyde, but shoppers hate to see that in their shampoo ingredients).

Fragrance is important because people like it and because —unlike everything else in shampoo—it is very hard for competitors to duplicate. A given fragrance may contain fifty or sixty materials, which you'll note are not identified. Sometimes a knockoff brand is exactly the same as a more expensive one, except that it smells like old cabbage water.

Quarternium-15 is a preservative. Keeps the shampoo from breaking down. I personally prefer Methylchloroisothiazolinone Methylisothiazolinone, because of the way it rolls off the tongue.

FD&C stands for the Food, Drug and Cosmetic Act of 1938, which requires that no dyes may be used in foods, drugs and cosmetics except those approved and numbered by Washington. The two dyes listed here make this shampoo green.

And there you have shampoo. From time to time new ingredients pop up. "We have to follow where the minor brands go," says John Corbett of Clairol, who is one of the two people who demystified shampoo for me. (The other is Lynn McMurtrie, who works for J.L. Prescott, which creates knockoffs.) "If one of them comes out saying pig's ears are great for hair, we have to say we have pig's ears. It's very frustrating."

The surfactant does just about all of what shampoo does that we like. It also does what we don't like: it leaves hair dry, hard to comb, unmanageable. (You try writing about hair products without sounding like a commercial.) There are two factors here:

1. Shampoo takes off too much of our old friend-or-enemy sebum. Sebum holds hair together, keeps moisture in and helps prevent the cuticle flakes from breaking, sticking out and making the hair surface irregular and tangly.

2. Shampoo imparts a negative electrical charge to hair. Hair doesn't conduct electricity, just holds it (and can transfer it to a comb so that a comb will pick up bits of paper). When every hair has a negative charge on it, hairs repel each other: the flyaway effect.

So we follow shampoo with conditioner. Conditioners didn't come in until the late fifties. They were called creme rinses then. Tame, manufactured by Gillette, was the first. Creme rinses gradually got thicker (folks got to have viscosity, so the product won't run through their fingers the way money does) and came to be called conditioners. (Now there is a trend to calling them "after-shampoo treatment," which I guess sounds more medical.) Conditioners are based on the principle, as John Corbett puts it, "that it's better to have nice clean dirt that we provide on your hair than nasty bug-filled dirt formed by your body."

Conditioners counteract the two ill effects of the surfactant in shampoo. They provide a little oiliness (that's where those marginal conditioners in the shampoo ingredients come in) to replace the sebum, and they dispel the electrical charge.

The oil may be from "the jojoba evergreen shrub," which at one point everybody in Hollywood was investing in, or it may be mineral oil, cottonseed oil, olive oil, corn oil, castor oil, sesame oil, soybean oil, egg oil (whatever that is) or safflower oil; or it may be a synthetic resin such as silicone or dimethicone; or mixtures of all these. Matter of taste.

Another lube factor in some conditioners is hydrolyzed animal protein, or collagen, whose effect is marginal but which does seem to bond well with damaged hair cuticles. Hydrolyzed animal protein is not obtained, as a Bible Belt preacher proclaimed recently, from minced human fetuses, but from animal hides—or, in some fancy but by no means necessarily better conditioners—animal placentas. Some conditioners claim that they contain actual keratin, the hair protein, but in fact keratin molecules are too large to bond with the hair shaft, and if they're broken down into amino acids so they will adhere, then they're just amino acids.

The main thing conditioner has is a good "quat," or quaternary ammonium compound. The most common ones are stearalkonium chloride and cetrimonium chloride. The quat

> **SOME NICE HAIR LINES—9**
>
> Lo! as that youth's eyes burned at thine, so went
> Thy spell through him, and left his straight neck bent
> And round his heart one strangling gold hair.
> —Dante Gabriel Rossetti, *The House of Life*

picks up the negative electrical charge and sends it out into the air, so that shampooed hair can live with itself. (According to Sarah Gilbert of Columbia, South Carolina, you can achieve the same effect by rubbing aluminum foil on your hair.)

Some other ingredients in some conditioners:

Allantoin. Supposed to help in "healing." But you can't heal hair. If your scalp is irritated, allantoin might help heal that. But at the level at which it's present in conditioner, don't count on it.

Kelp, grape skin, silk protein, mistletoe extract, oat flour, autolyzed yeast, cherry kernel oil. These add luster. To the packaging.

In the brief history of conditioners, there has been one big advance, or rather retreat. In the late 1970s Agree cream rinse appeared. It did, in fact, as advertised, "beat the greasies." That's because conditioner manufacturers had been throwing in so many new lubing substances (for instance, beeswax, paraffin and hydroxyethyl cellulose, which is an ingredient in wallpaper paste), and never taking any out, that conditioner had become too heavy. Agree cut back to a few oils. By that time people didn't want cream rinse anymore, so Agree was not a big hit, but it did bring the industry to its senses.

Not long ago *Consumer Reports* tested forty-seven different conditioners. "All were judged effective in reducing tangling and improving softness and shine." Prices ranged from ten cents to $1.52 an ounce. One of the cheapest, Suave Balsam and Protein Extra Body, was judged second best. The most expensive, Vidal Sassoon Extra Protection, was judged thirty-ninth.

Sebum is free.

BEWARE OF IMITATIONS

Bear's grease may be frowned upon as a hair dressing today, but as recently as the late nineteenth century it was chic enough (scented), and, when you think about it, it's never been all that easy to get ahold of. Sometimes rancid lard was offered as bear's grease by the unscrupulous. Honest slickum-mongers offered a bear's-grease substitute whose ingredients were:

½ pound huile de rose
½ pound huile de fleur d'orange
½ pound huile d'acacia
½ pound huile de tubereus
½ pound huile de jasmin
10 pounds almond oil
12 pounds lard
2 pounds acacia pomade
4 ounces otto of bergamot
2 ounces otto of cloves

LOOSE ENDS

● Hairdressing salons will try to sell you their own fancy brands. The great common distinction of these brands is their expensiveness.

● I am advised by Susan DiSesa of Pantheon Books that she once read somewhere that the second-most-printed phrase in English, after "Close Cover Before Striking," was "Lather, rinse, repeat." The first is good advice, the second bad. Unless you have something extremely yucky on your head (I'm told that WACs have to put baby oil on their hair so it will stay strictly in place), or unless you want to give more body to the profits of the shampoo companies, one shampooing is enough.

● After a while your hair gets tired of any given shampoo or conditioner, so you shouldn't stick with the same one for more than a month or so. Consumers know this. They are so disloyal to brands of shampoo and conditioner that dozens of different varieties—few of which last very long—are constantly struggling to hold a profitable share of the market. At one point not long ago, for $1.29 you could buy a bottle of Flex and a certificate that you could mail in for a refund of $1.50.

● Some conditioners are advertised as "self-adjusting." Ignore this.

● What dandruff shampoos do is cause the little flecks of scalp skin to stick together in large flecks, which come out in your comb instead of drifting onto your shoulders.

● Swedish for "manageable" is *handelbaar*.

THE FIRST HAIR

I said we would get around to Ronald Reagan, and now we do. You know of course he had his part changed from right to left by Warner Brothers right after he went to Hollywood. (Jimmy Carter changed his from right to left during his administration.)

But of course the big story is the color. Gerald Ford is supposed to have said once that Reagan's hair wasn't dyed, it was just prematurely orange. Probably the only Fordian quip.

The President's barber, Milton Pitts, steadfastly denies that the President dyes his hair. (Wouldn't you?) He does say he has talked the President into lowering his pompadour somewhat.

I have this to add. I talked to some people. People who work with someone who has actually worked with the President's hair. What these people told me is that it's true that the President does not dye his hair. But he does use a pomade that has a darkening effect.

One other thing I have in my notes. I read this somewhere. The President often has his valet rub his hair with Vaseline.

No, wait. That was Calvin Coolidge.

A SPOT OF COMFORT, FOR ELISHA

"…and as he was going up by the way, there came forth little children out of the city, and mocked him, and said unto him, Go up, thou bald head, go up, thou bald head. And he turned back, and looked on them, and cursed them in the name of the Lord. And there came forth two she bears out of the wood, and tare forty and two children of them."

—Second Kings

WHAT MY FRIEND DAN KLEIN HAS NOTED ABOUT THE EFFECT OF THE WEATHER ON HIS BALDING HEAD

"When it rains, it shines."

THEN THERE ARE THOSE WHO MOCK WIGS

My daughter Ennis knows a prep-school soccer player who got a punk haircut, offending his coach, who made him shave his head and wear a wig. The soccer player wears the wig so that the part is in the back.

SOME POPULAR STYLES IN INEXPENSIVE WIGS

Saturday Night Special
Disco Fever
Cloud Nine
Light and Airy
Nashville
Eva's Choice (Eva being Eva Gabor)

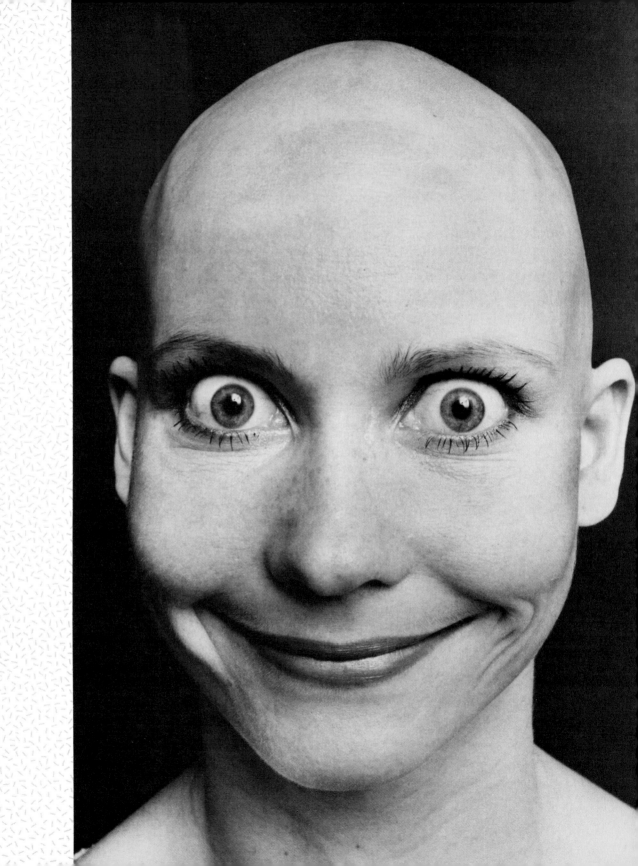

CHAPTER SEVEN
YOU KNOW HOW TO AVOID FALLING HAIR? STEP ASIDE

Some measures that have been tried, down through the ages, in the war against baldness:

►Equal parts of Abyssinian greyhound's heel, date blossoms and ass's hoof, boiled in oil

►Dog urine

►Spirits of rosemary and acetic acid

►Equal quantities of pigeon's dung and honey simmered together over a slow fire

►Equal parts fat of a lion, fat of a hippopotamus, fat of a crocodile, fat of a goose, fat of a snake and fat of an ibex

►Wortley's Berenizon: Peruvian balsam three parts, castor oil three parts, Spanish fly four parts, alcohol thirty-five parts and rosewater forty parts

►Oil of wormwood

►Spiderwebs

►Onion juice

►Mullein flowers

►Coconut fat, sulphur oil and oil of mustard

►Jerusalem artichoke juice

►The dew that fell from St. John's wort onto vegetation before daybreak on St. John's morning

Marika Blosfeldt chooses to be bald.

►Almond oil, ammonia, Spanish fly and lemon oil

►Bear's grease and laudanum

►Hedge garlic

►Feeding the patient seaweed, applying crude oil shampoo to his scalp, massaging his scalp, rubbing his head with garlic twice daily and every twelve days rubbing his head with lard and feeding him garlic

►Estrogen cream

►German army horse salve

►Something called Boro-Salicylate-Rosorcin, Newbro

►Glover's Sarcoptic Mange Cure

►Inositol, a B vitamin (After using this "one man of forty-eight, who had been bald for years, grew hair so thick that it looked like rabbit fur," wrote Adele Davis, the nutrition enthusiast. "Surprisingly enough, he was extremely proud of it.")

►Pulling the remaining hair until, with a distinct popping noise like that of popcorn popping, the scalp is lifted from the skull (People who survived being scalped by Indians reported hearing the same sound.)

►Allowing Liesel—a certain cow in West Germany for whose saliva restorative powers have been claimed—to lick the head, at fourteen dollars a lick

All of these cures have elicited enthusiastic testimonials. In 1948 Patricia M. Stenz, a redhead herself, ran a clinic at Hollywood and Vine that dispensed two solutions, one red and one white, that were supposed to make the scalp unpalatable to the fungus that she said caused baldness. Sure baldness ran in the family, she said: so did athlete's foot. Sons caught it from fathers. Her process was endorsed by Jimmy Stewart, Dick Powell, Gig Young and Gene Kelly. Yet male-pattern baldness, even in Hollywood (Burt Reynolds has resorted to a hairpiece, Jack Nicholson and Frank Sinatra to hair transplants), thrives.

"Short of castration," Jane Brody once wrote (startlingly, I thought) in the New York *Times*, "there is currently no safe and effective way to prevent or cure the most common kind of baldness." I guess castration *might* help, since baldness is believed to occur when one of the male hormones turns mean (as those hormones have been known to do) and starts causing follicles to retire from active, real-by-God-hair-producing life. (These follicles continue to produce tiny downy hairs that no one can see.) But let me say this right now, as a person who shows no disposition toward balding (and happens to feel a little tired this evening): Hippocrates—who may himself have been subject to hair loss, but we aren't sure—was wrong when he said bald men are "of an inflammatory habit; and the plasma in their head being agitated and heated by salacity, coming to the epidermis withers the roots of the hair causing it to fall off."

In other words—Picasso, Henry Miller and Marvin Hagler aside—baldness does not imply an abundance of male hormones. Any more than being a member of the Joint Chiefs of Staff does. It appears that many men's scalps are genetically disposed to screw up the relationship between hormone and follicle.

I wanted to get that straight. But I must say that no bald man has ever said to me, "Well, I guess *you'll* never get bald. Been castrated?" In fact, men with common male-pattern baldness break down into two categories: the ones who make no bones about it, and look clean and spry; and the ones who will go to any length—like parting the remaining hair at the back of the neck and bringing it way, way forward, as Ernest Hemingway did—to pretend that they are as furry as anybody. (Hemingway, it has recently been pointed out by biographers and critics, was always fooling with his hair in life and dwelling on hair in his work.) Trying to tell men in the second category that

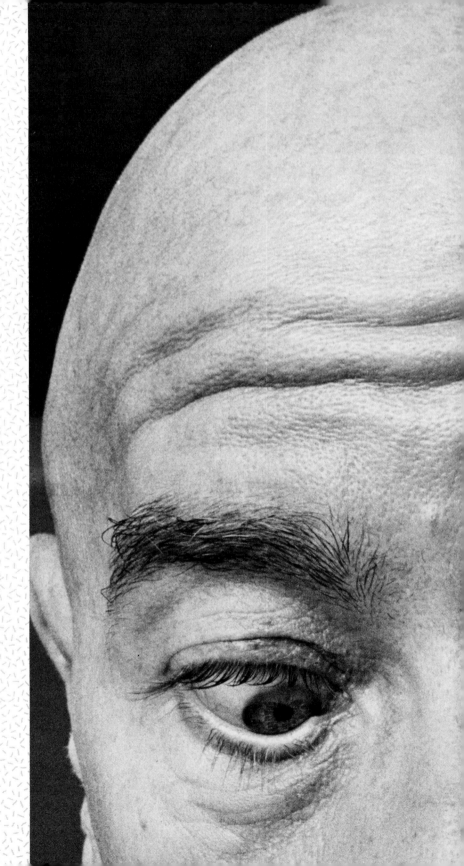

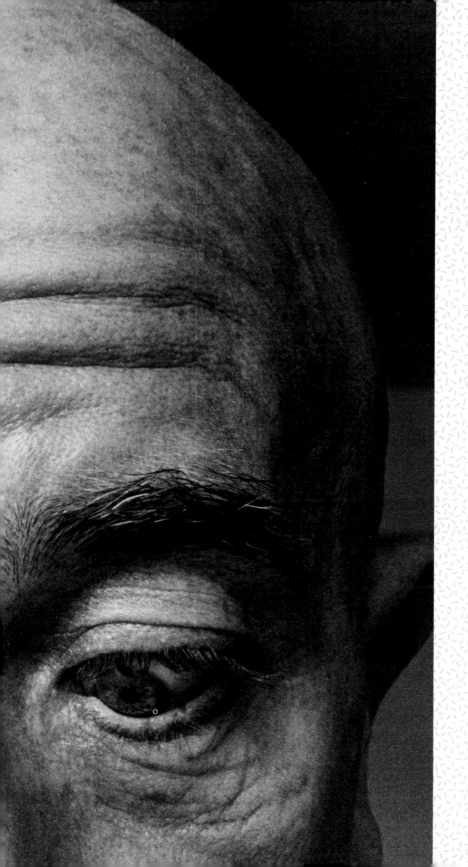

125

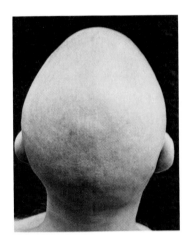

they look fine bald is like telling weight-conscious women that they look fine plump. They don't want to hear it.

Oh, I know John McEnroe once disputed a linesman's call by shouting at him, "Grow some hair!" I know that an old English term for a bald head was "a fly rink."

But what I think self-conscious balding men should do is reflect upon *alopecia areata universalis*, an as yet incurable disease that causes men, women and children to lose *all* their hair, from eyelids to pubes. At the age of fourteen, for example, a girl gradually loses all her head hair. Then it grows back. Then it all falls out again and so does all her body hair.

But people deal with it. Most of them begin to do so when they're girls and boys. Middle-aged guys with bald spots ought to read the *National Alopecia Areata Newsletter*. "The bargaining with God to at least have my eyelashes grow back." "Whenever I heard the word 'hair' I would freeze." "My hairpiece and the wind and my terrified outlook toward it." "In order to keep the other kids from pulling off my wig I would let them see it." "The unending question of 'Why does your hair always look so perfect?'" It is gratifying to read writers who *convincingly* always come around to the importance—the relief—of telling the truth. Here's a woman relating what happened when she was Xeroxing an article in a copy shop:

> The article has a picture of me with the heading, "How One Woman Coped With Her Baldness." Charming. The guy behind me in line for the machine said to me, "Oh, is that you?" It caught me off guard and I felt a little like someone had pulled down my pants in public. He then went on to tell me that his roommate of three years has *alopecia universalis*, and that this guy is great looking and gets all the girls, etc. I gave him a business card (hey, I'm no dummy) and told him to have his roommate give me a call.

It can't be easy. Having no hair must be a little like having no pants, and wearing no hair that's rooted must be like wearing pants that you imagine people can see through or that you are afraid may drop at any moment. Big kids pull down little kids' pants.

But everybody—particularly the big kid who pulls down little kids' pants—is a little naked kid in some regard. I have been sitting here for some time thinking about this, and now I'm going to say it, because I think it's true: courage—kicking ass in a life-enhancing way—always involves going ahead and owning up to being that little naked kid.

If you are a bald guy who can't stand to read the *National Alopecia Areata Newsletter*, there are less profound ways in which you can buck yourself up. You can try rubbing minoxidil on your pate. Minoxidil is a drug originally designed to help people with extremely high blood pressure. For reasons that are not understood, many of these people began to become more hirsute. And it appears that maybe 30 percent of men with common baldness can regain some ground if they rub minoxidil on their scalps every day for the rest of their lives.

If you can find a doctor to prescribe minoxidil, you can try it at a cost of about a thousand dollars a year, and it may work, and it may not have other side effects. (Then again, recent studies indicate, it may.) The USDA may approve the sale of it over the counter, which would make it less expensive. Or you can have plugs of hair sewn into your scalp. Or you can have a big strip of bald scalp peeled away and the still-hairy parts of your scalp stretched to cover the gap—in which case you have to be a little tentative about bending over to tie your shoes.

Or you can tell yourself this: that the best men always come out on top.

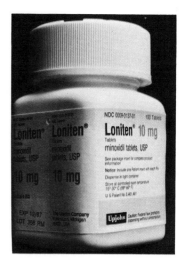

WIGMAKER
RAFFAELE

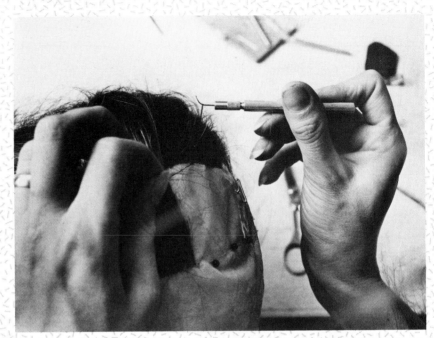

"I'm the best wigmaker in the world," says Raffaele Mollica. "I charge sixteen hundred and fifty dollars and I've got people waiting six months."

His clients are women who have lost all their own hair. "When that happens to a woman, it's worse I think than losing five fingers. Guy makes a move on her, her wig flies off, he says, 'What is this?' Guy can hardly look at her.

"I actually make heads of hair. I get as close to God as any man, but I couldn't if I didn't have the hair. I use the best human hair, from the southern region of Italy, where I come from. I've got connections. Hair that never sees the sun. From women who work in the fields with kerchiefs over their heads. We spend a month working on this wig one strand at a time. It goes through my hands, my wife's hands, assistants' hands. The netting is all silk-lined.

"You've got to educate the women who come in here. Teach them how to comb it, how to wear it, how to wash it. Just think of a garment you could wear every day!

"I kiss about a hundred and fifty people a week.

Give 'em that squeeze which is not your regular squeeze —a little extra to reaffirm them. Cause they've given up on themselves aesthetically. I do that right in front of my wife.

"It's psychology until they don't listen to you; then you have to scream at them, call them names. I dominate every one of my clients. That's what they need. They're trying to dominate me to see if they got the right guy. Let them do that and you've lost 'em. It's a matter of what I know and what they know. They only call on me when everything else fails. Cause I cost more."

IF YOU THINK
YOU HAVE HAIR PROBLEMS...

...you should read *Anomalies and Curiosities of Medicine*, a book first published in 1896.

"There was a record in the last century of a boy of sixteen who ate all the hair he could find; after death his stomach and intestines were almost completely lined with hairy masses."

In 1842 "a medical student...complained of dyspepsia and a sticky sensation in the mouth. On examination a considerable growth of hair was found on the surface of the tongue. The hair would be detached in vomiting but would grow again, and when he was last seen they were one inch long."

Okay! Okay! Wait a minute! The rest of these cases have happy endings. I promise. I wouldn't share them with you if they didn't. In what follows, "D" stands for downside, "U" for upside.

D: "A girl of twenty with a large abdominal swelling was admitted to a hospital. Her illness began five years previously, with frequent attacks of vomiting [there will be no more vomiting, I guarantee], and on three occasions it was noticed that she became quite bald. Abdominal section was performed, the stomach opened, and from it was removed a mass of hair which weighed five pounds and three ounces."

U: "A good recovery ensued."

D: In the late nineteenth century a woman was exhibited as "the lady with a mane." She had, well, a mane of long black hair growing from the center of her back.

U: In the photograph she and the mane look nice.

D: A man named Blake had a full coat of hair from just above his navel to just below his knees, all around.

U: When Blake was dressed, you couldn't see any of this. When he was undressed, it looked like he was wearing "bathing tights."

D: "A woman of twenty-four, having white skin and hair of deep black,...after a long illness...became covered, especially on the back, breast and abdomen, with a multitude of small elevations similar to those which appear on exposure to cold. These little elevations became brownish at the end of a few days, and short, fair, silky hair was observed on the summit of each, which grew so rapidly that the whole surface of the body with the exception of the hands and face became..."

U: "...velvety. The hair thus evolved was afterward thrown out spontaneously and was not afterward reproduced."

D: *Pilica polonica* is a condition first noted as widespread in Poland at about the year 1285. It affected about 7.5 percent of the peasantry and beggars, and about 5 percent of the nobility and burghers. "A clammy and agglutinating sweat... occurred over the cranium, the hair became unctuous, stuck together, and appeared distended with an adhesive matter of reddish-brown color.... The hair was so acutely sensitive that the slightest touch occasioned severe pain at the roots. A viscid matter of a very offensive smell, like that of spoiled vinegar, or according to Rayer like that of mice or garlic, exuded from the whole surface of each affected hair. This matter glued the hairs together, at first from their exit at the skin, and then along the entire length; it appeared to be secreted from the whole surface of the scalp and afterward dried into an incrustation.... The hair was matted and stuck together in a variety of ways, so as to resemble ropes.... Sometimes these masses united together and formed one single thick club like the tail of a horse.... Again, and particularly in females, the hair would become matted and glued together into one uniform intricate mass of various magnitudes. The hair of the whole body was likely to be attacked with this disease." And here I draw a veil. Except to say that many of the common folk believed that if you cut off this matted hair, you'd get apoplexy and epilepsy and die. So they went around in this condition until the end of their days.

U: Over the centuries Poles began to wash themselves more and to wear more ventilated headdresses, and by 1896 *pilica polonica* was quite rare.

D: "Rayer saw a Piedmontese of twenty-eight, with an athletic build, who had but little beard or hair on the trunk, but whose scalp was covered with a most extraordinary crop. It was extremely fine and silky, was artificially frizzled, dark brown in color, and formed a mass nearly five feet in circumference."

U: There is no indication that the Piedmontese considered this a problem.

CHAPTER EIGHT
STREET HAIR
NEW YORK

Yours may only mumble, trail off, or go, "Aw, don't mind *me*," but everybody's hair speaks, and some people's hair gets right out into the street and raises a hue and cry.

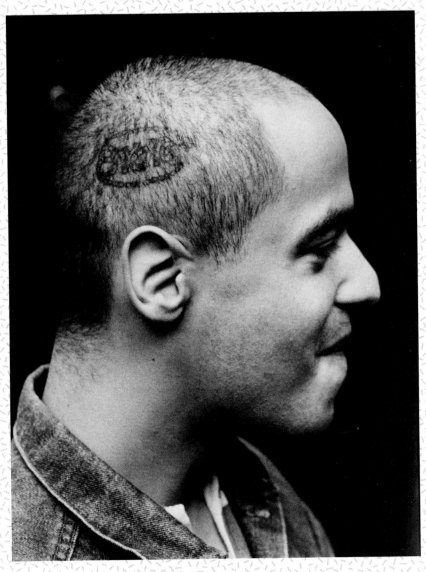

The statement Won Variano makes through his hair is political. "I don't believe in hair," he says. "I think it's just a phony thing, to go pay twenty dollars for a haircut." So he keeps his shaved down to quarter-inch stubble, through which you can read a tattoo: "Psychos," the name of the band he plays in.

"This is the American way, American style, clean-cut American," he says. "I'm ready to pick up a gun and fight for this country because it's the best place in the whole world."

He has no interest in the armed services as such, however. Nor in the organized American economy. "I wouldn't want to pose for you if you're going to use it for commercial purposes. You'll do a book, make money out of it, then I'll be commercially exploited and I'm against that."

What if we gave him a dollar?

"Okay."

Cheryl Rixon has a yard or so of twined and flourishing mermaid hair, which she calls "a lure that works." She does her hair herself.

"I don't want it to look too much like a hairdo."

What does she want it to look like?

"A tantrum."

133

Joe and Cliff are Rogue Animals, though they are wearing patches that say "Legion of Doom" and "Casket Crew." The Rogue Animals have a headquarters nearby that has a dungeon in it, but when asked if they will submit to being photographed they shrug graciously.

"Want me to comb it?" Joe asks. "Lots of snags in it from riding the bike."

Occasionally they are asked to appear in movies. "I was in *Album Slave* and completely forgot about it," says their friend Merrill, who has bones in her hair.

What are those bones, exactly?

"Some dog ribs a friend gave me."

So. Are Joe and Cliff making a statement with their shoulder-length hair?

"I wouldn't know what to say about that," says Joe.

STREET HAIR
LONDON

Hair in the eighties has so many options! It can be stylishly down to the coccyx or stylishly just long enough to have the texture of plush. It can be one of those lengths on one side of the head and the other on the other. It can defy gravity. It can be rigidly fluffy. It can be chartreuse.

When possibility ferments so, there is always the temptation just to be trimmed (except far more expensively) like a person applying for a job at a bank in Moline, Illinois, in 1958. "People have been interesting for so long—maybe the next step is to be dull and boring," says a London hairdresser.

But there is still plenty of hair around that reaches toward the cutting edge by crying out, "I am this strange stuff, *hair*! I have had extraordinarily unnatural things done to me!"

It may be a Mohawk strip seven inches high, colored black and gold and green with peacock-wing eyes, worn by a young man who also wears a can of hairspray around his neck like a talisman. Or it may be what looks like a fifties ratted style gone out of whack: the embarrassing gap between what's teased and what's not—the hole in the bouff—is paraded. Or a person may give the appearance that he or she has been held down by bullies wielding dull razors, spray paint and shears. In the days of Marie Antoinette fashionable hair was an unholy mess but looked like it wasn't. Now it looks like it's an unholy mess but it isn't; or anyway the mess is carefully contrived.

Over the last twenty years or so, hairstyles have tended to derive from adolescents in the street. In the hippie era luxuriant hair-down-to-here covered pimples or drew the eye away from them. Punk hair exposes acne; it's the aesthetic equivalent of unabashed bad skin. The New Wave has been co-opted now to the point that women in New York opt for "Park Avenue punk": a traditionally elegant cut with here or there a mock-ugly tuft. But on King's Road, in the Chelsea district of London, dated but dogged hard-core punks still gather. Their hair is a rude joke that complements their spotty skin and their economic fecklessness. They're on the dole, they charge a pound to pose for tourists' cameras, and they vaguely have in mind forming rock bands with names like Anthrax. (The Dead Kennedys are *nostalgia* now.)

Hippie hair flowed down toward oneness with nature. Punk hair—kept up originally with sugar-water, now with state-of-the-art hairspray—projects upward in pointless pointy spires. The key word in the slogans daubed on the heavy, ratty, black leather jackets is "Chaos."

The punks on display on King's Road are an affable enough lot if you give them their pound and pass a little time with them. I talked to one who was quite affectionate toward his cheerful black and white dog, whose name was Anarchy.

CHAPTER NINE
PULLING IT ALL TOGETHER: THE HAIR THEORY OF HUMAN EVOLUTION

I am not going to announce this with a great deal of fanfare. I am not a scientist, nor a registered cosmetologist, so the evolution and hair establishments may well react to my Hair Theory of Human Evolution the way people in general react when I tell them I am writing a book about hair. They may well just look at me funny.

But it has come to me, why people have hair. And that revelation has unraveled, to my satisfaction, the mystery of human evolution.

Scientists are always trying to say what man is, exclusively. The animal that laughs? The animal that uses symbols? The animal that reflects upon its selfhood? The animal that could blow up the world?

Any of these distinctions will serve, up to a point. None of them gets down to root causes. *Why* is man what he is? You can't just say, "Well, I guess he's just that kind of guy." That begs the question.

I'll tell you what man is. And at the same time I'll tell you what made him all the other things he is.

It hit me when I was looking through *An Illustrated Dictionary of Hairdressing and Wigmaking*. And came to this illustration:

Natural
disposition
of
head hair.

We are always trying to achieve "natural-looking" hair. But by that we don't mean what nature, or hair, intends. If we didn't fool with our hair we would all, more or less (some of us less wavily, some more frizzily), look like that illustration. And no other animal would. Not even the sheepdog.

Man is the animal that is always trying to keep her hair out of her eyes. And out of her way generally. And failing.

I don't see that there can be any argument with that.

Now. The implications.

What was the one crucial step that commenced man's ascent from lower-animal status? Evolutionists tend to agree: the transition from going on all fours to standing erect. When some snuffling prehominid got up on its hind legs and stayed there, the whole messy human thing began to fall into place. To make a long story short, this animal started relating to its environment by sight instead of by smell; an enormous new range of information opened up; the brain expanded to take it in; the front feet were freed to develop into hands; the hands and brain advanced together as they contrived tools, manufacture, agriculture.

I didn't work this out myself. It is widely accepted.

But. What caused that prehominid to stand erect? It just took a notion? "Took a notion" won't get it in evolutionary theory. There has to be a genetic fluke, which confers an evolutionary advantage, and therefore perpetuates itself. Nothing in the fossils can tell us what that mutation was.

That's because it was something that doesn't fossilize. It was hair.

This animal stood erect because it was born with a wild hair, or rather with a headful of them. A headful of follicles out of control. As this animal grew, the fur on its head grew all out of proportion.

With hair like that, how are you going to snuffle around like a normal animal? Hair that long gets in the way of your nose, your eyes, your mouth, your feet.

So you are always tossing your head back. The longer your hair gets, the more you have to shift your weight to your haunches to throw it back. And then you start kicking at it with your front feet. And the next thing you know, you are standing up. You walk on your rear feet, and with your front ones you hold your hair back.

But you don't want half your feet to be tied up in constant hair care. As it happens, all that hair has shielded your cranium so that your brain has relaxed and grown slightly larger than the other animals'. Which gets you thinking: maybe you could use a sharp rock to cut off some of this hair. And you could use some reeds to tie it back. Now you've got an implement, and something bordering on clothes. Also, you're holding a part of your own body that you have detached, by means of technology. That's pretty heavy: you've cut part of yourself off. That part develops symbolic importance. Something creepy about it, but powerful.

I can't be certain that the reason you look into a reflecting pool for the first time is to check out your hair. But fooling with your hair gives you something to do *while* you're looking into a reflecting pool; gives you a reason to linger there. And the whole notion of face begins to dawn on you. Face and self. Your fur having all run to the top of your head, there isn't much of it on your face, or on your descendants' faces. Your grandchildren notice that their mother's face is very smooth and shows subtle emotions. The human smile comes in, the human scowl, the human moue. Here's what gets the first laugh: Mama holding her hair (which you love to touch) over her eyes (which have it for you), and then parting her hair and saying, "Peek-a-boo."

Now you've got language.

The babies are so hairless they have to be cuddled, swaddled, bundled up far longer than the young of other species, and therefore they have time to daydream, mope, deplore the older generation and experiment with their hair for years before they are thrust out into the world.

The female hominid is smaller; the male can grab her by the hair and drag her, so he does. She and her face specialize in expressing emotions, like "Turn me loose, you big ape!"

You big what? It just popped out. Once it's said, the male can't quite get it off his mind. He's *not* a big ape? Or he's not supposed to be one? What is the point, exactly? Why carry on so? It's that emotional stuff. But he remembers liking emotion in his mother's face. What was that thing she used to do with her hair . . . ?

So what the heck, he turns loose of the female's hair. And jumps on her. "Oh, great!" she says. "You drag me around, and then you expect me . . . I have a headache. Will you never understand . . . ?"

Smooth faces! Can't live with them, can't live without them. The smoother a female's face, and body, the more likely she is to be selected, protected and have children plopped in her lap. She passes on her smoothness. Gradually even males are bred, nurtured and thrown for loops in the direction of smoothness. (The top of some males' heads, in fact, overreacts, and since it is only bald men who are bothered by baldness, many women pick bald men and perpetuate baldness.) But the male still devotes most of his time to what he does best: fighting and lurching around, running through brush and threatening other males; so facial and body hair retain survival value for him. (Alex Karras, the former football great, has said he quailed, when he was a little kid, at the notion of tackling older guys with hairy legs.)

It's hard to deal with your hair by yourself. Hominids groom each other. Social relationships develop. Certain members of the community (later they will be known as witch doctors, still later as hairdressers) invent stylings and baldness cures.

With their hair up and back, people look up and around. Man, whom Plato called "the plumeless biped," can see great distances through the air; can see stars; but since he has hair instead of feathers he can't get up there. Man builds aircraft. Man gets up there, looks down and builds nuclear weaponry, the only thing that can undo everything that wild hair has caused: civilization.

That is the Hair Theory of Human Evolution. Like hair itself, it pretty well covers, or at least puts a ring around, all the most important points.

It explains why we have hair and why hair is so fascinating. You know how you feel when you see someone with hair in her eyes? You want to push it back. That's a deep evolutionary urge. Our own hair we are always sweeping back, combing back, tucking back and doing *up*: roached, lifted, teased, haloish, bouffant, spiked, winged, piled, coiled, bouncy, af-roed, Pre-Raphaelitized, twined, fluffy, pouffed, topknotted, stuffed and mounted, pompadoured, blown, bobbed, flat-topped, parted, foo-fooed, moussed. Anything but lank. Anything but hanging. Anything but the way it is naturally disposed to be.

Left to its own devices (one of which is sebum), hair grows down, all the way around. And when it decides to, it falls out. It doesn't want to look nice, by our standards. But here's the thing: if hair had looked like a permanent to begin with, we wouldn't have any standards. We'd still be on all fours snuffling.

Hair just wants to be powerful. It wants us to remember where we were before it picked us up, by the strength of its perversity.

Vexed, and knowing it will grow back, we try to show it who's boss. We have it cut, with trepidation, and as we see it fall we are uneasy, because in those swatches, over which the hairdresser-shaman holds sway, we see human inertia and potential: peculiar, bestial, provocative, recalcitrant, always beyond us, always right handy. The Indian god Shiva, representing the creative and sexual energy of the universe, is always depicted with masses of long, tangled, piled-up hair on his head.

And if that isn't anthropomorphism all over. You think if birds, bees or violets could depict the creative and sexual energy of the universe they would depict it with a lot of hair on it?

No. It's just us. There are so many other things we could be seeing, in so many unhairy terms, but our hair keeps getting in our eyes. "Look at me!" it cries. "I'm coming loose! I'm drooping! There's a photographer! Look at me!" And we do.

We are like the effete prince in the Monty Python movie, whose father gestures expansively toward the palace window, which overlooks the kingdom. "Son," the king says, "some day all this will be yours."

The prince replies, with delight, "You mean the *drapes*?"

MAKEOVER

Here is the intrinsically great-looking Wendy Gervasi. Her hair, here, is not really adding anything, is it? Her hair seems almost embarrassed to be here. "I look young here, and sort of dumb," is Wendy's opinion.

And yet her hair, in hiding, exposes her high brow. A high brow is a sign of a highly evolved human being.

However, a highly evolved human being wants to *do something* with her hair. Paul Hauch of Glemby at the Plaza in New York is going to make Wendy's hair over. And with her hair, her.

Why can't humanity leave well enough alone?

Here's why humanity can't leave well enough alone. Here is Wendy's hair in a state of nature. Anyway, a washed state of nature. Here is what hair will do, if we leave it alone. Hair will swallow not only the human brow but almost all the rest of the human face. Walk around like this for a while and the next thing you know you're not walking. You're down on all fours subsisting on whatever you can locate with your nose and mouth.

Humanity won't let that happen to Wendy Gervasi.

Here we have hot rollers. They produce tight curls, which have to be brushed out into just such a looseness as looks sort of messy but clearly isn't.

Now Wendy could be an empress, a courtesan, a country music queen, the hit of a charity gala. Thanks to hundreds of years of advances in hair culture. And because she is intrinsically great-looking. And because she has an abundance of hair that wants to be limp but can be dissuaded.

153

GLOSSARY

Arrectores pilorum: The small involuntary muscles at the hair follicles that cause hair to stand on end.

Arslock: The end of a lock of hair farthest from the head (seventeenth century).

Baby: The small curl on the tail of a judge's wig.

Baffona: Italian for a woman with a not too unpleasant mustache.

Bouff: To bouff the hair, or to bouff it up, is to foo-foo it.

Bromidrosis capitis: A condition which causes the hair to stink.

Canities: Gray hair.

Cejijunto: Spanish for a person with one long continuous eyebrow.

Chase-me-Charlie: A kiss curl.

Cincinni: The hair hanging behind the ears.

Clitpole: A head of frizzy or tangled hair. In Dorset and Somerset. Only.

Comma curl: A curl shaped like a comma.

Eugene: "I'm off to get my hair eugened," in the 1920s, meant that you were off to have it permanent-waved by a system invented by Eugene Suter, which never quite caught on the way marcelling, invented by Marcel Grateau, did in the 1880s.

Ehestandswinkel: German for incipient balding at the temples.

Fly rink: A bald head (slang).

Follow-me-lads: Curls hanging over the shoulders.

Foo-foo: To foo-foo (also, sometimes, to foo) the hair is to fluff it up.

Frizette: A cluster of small curls, usually artificial, worn above and on the forehead.

Furfurration: The falling of dandruff from the scalp.

Goatene: A pointed tuft which sticks straight up from the top of a woman's head as a goatee sticks down from a man's chin.

Hair finger: The middle finger of the right hand, which, since it is more sensitive than the index finger, is used by hair dealers, with the thumb, to feel the texture of hair.

Hairgrips (also **Kirby grips** and **hair-slides**): British for bobby pins.

Hairitorium: A place that sells wigs.

Hirci: Armpit hair, also called axillary hair, which lacks *arrectores pilorum*, and aren't you glad?

Juba: The hair on the back of the head.

Lanugo: Down, which covers the human fetus and persists throughout life, even on bald heads.

Misopogon: One who hates beards.

Misplaced eyebrow: A thin mustache (slang).

Native trisulphide of arsernium arsenicum flavum: You're on your own.

Occipito frontalis: The muscle of the head that can move the scalp.

Onchyphagy: Nail-biting (This belongs here because, a., fingernails are, like hair, excrescences of the epidermis and because, b., of manicurists.)

Orpiment: Native trisulphide of arsenium arsenicum flavum.

Philosity: The degree of body hair.

Pogonophobia: Morbid (as opposed to rational, healthy) fear of beards.

Pompadoodle: Cross between pompadour and poodle, i.e., a tightly curly hairdress swept up and back from the front.

Poor man's peruke: A wig consisting of just an old hunk of sheepskin or calfskin with the wool or hair on.

Queer flash: A miserable weatherbeaten wig (eighteenth century).

Rhusma: A dangerous Asian depilatory made of orpiment and unslaked lime.

Scalpette: Covering for a female bald spot.

Schnurbartbinde: German for a mustache-trainer, which is not a person but a band tied around the head that holds the mustache in such a position as you have in mind for it.

Scurf: British for dandruff. Said to be a prerequisite for the diplomatic corps.

Thesaurosis: Accumulation of hair-spray products in the lungs.

Tragedy head: Eighteenth-century theatrical wig suitable for tragic character.

Tragus: Ear hair.

Trichoptilosis: Split ends.

Vuzz poll: A head of untidy hair.

Whoops-a-daisy: Straight hair gathered into a casual spray at the top of the head.

Wild boar's back: Man's eighteenth-century wig style.

Woof: The cuttings from one head of hair (nineteenth century).

Xyster: Not, as students of football strategy might think, a defensive oyster, but rather an instrument used by medieval barber-surgeons to shave and scrape bones.

Zàzzera: Italian for the hair that grows on the back of the neck.

Zebedeen: One who shaves himself (nineteenth century).

QUESTIONS FOR FURTHER STUDY

(Answers on page 158)

1. In "The Gift of the Magi," considering that a watch won't grow back, who got the better deal?
2. In the glossary, which two terms did I make up?
3. How many hairs does the average human scalp hold?
4. Who starred in *The Boy with Green Hair*, and what was it about?
5. Are there any other neat hair stories from the history of England involving decapitation?
6. What is the best head of hair in the history of the movies?
7. Where did Elvis get his hairstyle?
8. How did a Fijian jungle fighter with the Allied forces in the South Pacific inform someone that his commanding officer had gone to the barbershop?
9. Can you grow hair on a billiard ball?
10. Are there any hair anecdotes that this would be a good place to sneak into the book?
11. Come on, there must be one more.
12. Has Slick Lawson in Nashville had any observations concerning hair?
13. Couldn't the baldness chapter have shown more sympathy toward balding men?

14. Why do some people have blue hair?

15. Is there any product that straightens kinky hair without lye?

16. Why do holy men always have either really long hair or hardly any?

17. How did the goddess Isis control the weather?

18. Where did the expression "to make a clean breast" come from?

19. How long does a hair live?

20. What happens to the hair on the floor of barbershops and hairdressers'?

21. Why do you see black youths wearing shower caps?

22. What did Ralph Kramden say when Alice asked him why she had to steam his raccoon hat over the teakettle before he could go to a meeting of the International Order of the Friendly Raccoons?

23. Whose hair defies all explanation?

24. Who was Ivan Peter Alexis Knoutscheffschlerwitz?

25. Isn't dust largely hair?

Answers ⟶

ANSWERS TO QUESTIONS FOR FURTHER STUDY

1. This was a question that arose on New Year's morning, and was never quite resolved.
2. *Goatene* and *whoops-a-daisy*. I tried to think of one for "toe hair," which a woman I know says she shaves, but it's hard because the Latin for "toe" is the same as the Latin for "finger."
3. Exactly 100,000, but who's counting?
4. Dean Stockwell, Pat O'Brien, Robert Ryan, prejudice.
5. In *The Private Life of Henry VIII*, Merle Oberon as Anne Boleyn, at her last hairdresser's appointment: "Will the net hold my hair together when my head falls?"
6. Oh, come on. Elsa Lanchester's in *The Bride of Frankenstein*.
7. Speculation has centered upon Tony Curtis, but in *Elvis and Gladys* Elaine Dundy argues convincingly (to my mind) that it was Captain Marvel, Jr.
8. "Him fella go get lawn mower belong 'm head."
9. No, it would slow down the game.
10. Well, Garrison Keillor told me one about going downstairs to this basement barbershop and there was just this one incredibly old barber there, no other barbers, no other customers. . . . It was a town where he'd never been before. He didn't want to turn and leave. . . . I think it would work best on the radio.
11. Well, there's one George Kimball told me, but you'd probably have to have seen Mike Katz, the sportswriter. Katz is an extremely hairy person—head, face, as far as the eye can see. Once Katz walked into a hotel barbershop and the barber took one look at him and said, "Not in here, buddy."
12. Yes. "In the sixties the intelligentsia grew their hair long, then all the proletarians started doing it and the intelligentsia cut theirs back and left that other bunch looking worse than they ever did. Nothing in the world makes long hair look longer than a hard hat. Now you've got all these thirty-five- and forty-year-old women going around with punk cuts, and I've figured out what those are. Those are ex-Geraldine Ferraro cuts. All these women did their hair like Geraldine Ferraro

and then she went out of favor and all their daughters started looking at them strange. And the only way they could go was shorter."

13. TV producer Mike Sullivan: "I had no idea I was going bald until I was at a job interview, and I saw the man was writing, 'Mike Sullivan, 26, balding.' Afterwards I stopped at a service station and went to the men's room and looked in the mirror, and aged ten years." Two women told me of men they knew who'd had hair transplants. One said, "His hair was always *bleeding*. He couldn't go outside." The other said, "When I got up close, his scalp looked like a Barbie doll's."

14. According to Kay Elder of Farah's Beauty School in Columbia, South Carolina, "Some people like it blue. It's meant to take the yellow out of white hair. But the older they get, the more they like it the bluer it gets."

15. No. And any product that claims to is telling what is known as the no-lye lie.

16. So as not to look like a TV preacher.

17. By braiding her hair or letting it down.

18. From the practice of shaving the chests of male witches, believed to make them confess.

19. A head hair, four or five years. A finger hair, 147 days.

20. Most of it is thrown out, but some is sold to gardeners, who put it around their plots to keep deer away. Occasionally a hairdresser will save a particularly nice swatch and sell it to a wigmaker.

21. It holds the moisture in their Geri-curls, those little tendrils like Michael Jackson wears.

22. "Because it makes the fur stand up like a crewcut."

23. Jack Lord's, on *Hawaii Five-O*.

24. A Siberian hairdresser in London in the eighteenth century. He filled the "hollows of the hair with soft aromatic herbs which prevent the disagreeable effect of that perspiration now so generally complained of." He would make a lady's head look like the head of a lion or wolf or any other animal she requested, or he would color it chestnut, blue, crimson or green.

25. A British expression for dust was "slut's wool." Sexist, of course.